and did he stop
and speak to you?

BY THE SAME AUTHOR

Non-Fiction: Monogram
              Another Part of the Forest
              Trumpet Voluntary
              Benefits Forgot
              A Name to Conjure With
              He Wrote Treasure Island
              All in Good Time
              The Way it Worked Out

Fiction: No Son of Mine
              The Woman in the Hall
              Little Red Horses
              Ten Days of Christmas
              Seventy Times Seven
              For All We Know

G. B. STERN

and did he stop and speak to you?

CHICAGO · 1958

HENRY REGNERY COMPANY

FOR IAN AND MEGAN DALRYMPLE

ACKNOWLEDGMENTS

Extracts from *Lytton Strachey* (The Rede Lecture 1943) by Sir Max Beerbohm quoted by permission of Lady Beerbohm, and the Cambridge University Press.

Extract from *A Christmas Garland* by Sir Max Beerbohm by permission of Lady Beerbohm, and Messrs. William Heinemann Ltd.

Poems from *A Few Late Chrysanthemums* and *Selected Poems* by John Betjeman quoted by permission of the Author, and Messrs. John Murray (Publishers) Ltd.

Extracts from unpublished poems by John Betjeman by permission of the Author.

Extracts from *Selina is Older*, *The Children's Summer* and *Quartet in Heaven* by Sheila Kaye-Smith by permission of Messrs. Cassell & Co. Ltd.

Quotation from *The Weald of Kent & Sussex* by Sheila Kaye-Smith by permission of Messrs. Robert Hale Ltd.

Extracts from *The Long Sunset* and *King John's Treasure* by R. C. Sherriff by permission of the Author, and Elek Books Ltd.

Extracts from *The Narrow Corner* and *The Painted Veil* by W. Somerset Maugham, and from the Preface to the Uniform Edition of his works quoted by permission of the Author, and Messrs. William Heinemann Ltd.

Quotations from *The History of Mr. Polly* by H. G. Wells by permission of the Executors of the late H. G. Wells.

Quotation from *Requiem* by Humbert Wolfe by permission of Miss Anne Wolfe, and Ernest Benn Ltd.

Extract from *Design for Living* by Noel Coward by permission of the Author.

Parts of the article on Somerset Maugham have appeared in *John o' London's Weekly* and in *The Sketch* magazine.

The article on the Lunts has appeared previously in *Drama*, the journal of the British Drama League.

Much of the material of the article on Sheila Kaye-Smith has appeared previously in *The Tablet*.

Extracts from G. B. Stern's own books *Monogram*, *Benefits Forgot* and *Another Part of the Forest* by permission of Messrs. Cassell & Co. Ltd.

CONTENTS

and did he stop

and speak to you?

Ah, did you once see Shelley plain,
   And did he stop and speak to you,
And did you speak to him again?
   How strange it seems, and new!

But you were living before that,
   And you are living after;
And the memory I started at—
   My starting moves your laughter.

I crossed a moor with a name of its own
   And a certain use in the world no doubt,
Yet a hand's-breadth of it shines alone
   'Mid the blank miles round about:

For there I picked up on the heather
   And there I put inside my breast
A moulted feather, an eagle-feather!
   Well, I forget the rest.

"AND DID YOU SPEAK TO HIM AGAIN?"

HAD Browning simply called his poem "A Memory," I should not have been despot enough to quote it robbed of its title; but because, poor fellow, he could never be altogether simple, he called it "Memorabilia"; yet even so, he could not spoil it. I daresay exact research would yield up plentiful data of how old or young he was when he met Trelawney, the original of Byron's Corsair; and stammering with eagerness and excitement, hardly able to articulate in the awe of discovering that this elderly man, this piratical fellow with the bushy beard and the bright dark eyes had actually once, years and years ago, seen Shelley and spoken to him—A torrent of questions, and then an incredulous: "But you were living before that happened, and you went on living afterwards, just as though—just as though—" And Trelawney looking down at him, laughing: "Well, why not, my boy? Shelley was just a man, you know, like the rest of us!"

Only it appears not to have been Trelawney, though Research Superficial declared for him on dates and geographical opportunity. Beware of the evidence of these if not allied to Research Psychological: Trelawney and Browning did indeed meet at Leghorn in 1844, twenty-two years after Shelley's death and when Robert Browning himself was over thirty; thus far and no further; the rest is on a wrong note; Trelawney, Shelley's intimate for that whole memorable summer at Pisa, would never have let fall a remark to cause any young man to imagine he had only seen Shelley *once*— "and did he stop and speak to you? and did you speak to him again?" —and Browning at thirty would already have grown out of the phase to produce that kind of touching reaction. Nor would Trelawney have laughed at it.

Fascinated by the poem itself, I had (like most people) been familiar with the first line for fifty years and more, without ever bothering to read it until recently; then indeed, for the theme of hero-worship goes deep with me, I did at last delve into the matter for confirmation of the span of years separating Shelley's death from Browning's birth, to make sure that the ardent boy could not himself have encountered his hero. But Shelley had lived in exile for most of Robert's childhood; and the tragic news of his drowning would hardly have affected a lad of ten who had lit upon the "Ode to a Skylark," perhaps, or learnt it at school as most of us did before we were ready for it and mixed him up with Keats and stumbled over the line "profuse strains of unpremeditated art." And say that in his adolescence he fell in love with "Prometheus Unbound" and "Adonais" . . . Seventeen? Eighteen? Twenty? Yes, I think about twenty when in a room full of people someone remarked casually: "That time when I met Shelley

and he said—" and there the young man burst in with
—well, with "Memorabilia."

Of course he did not write it then; on conjecture, years
passed (exact research would have enlightened me as to
how many) before in an indulgent mood—and also maybe
a little sadly, with a strain of nostalgia for his vanished
youth—he set down his emotions on suddenly meeting a
man who had once seen Shelley, spoken with him, heard
his voice, marked how his eye had kindled . . . Remembered and set down, too, his boyish fury and sense of dese-
cration that this casual stranger had dared have a separate
life of his own before he met Shelley, and another life
after. Why, everything else should have led up to that
supreme moment, and all the years afterwards been blank
and vacant except for that moment! But now, in his mature reconstruction of the incident, Browning himself a
famous poet and escaped into Christianity from the influence of Shelley's passionate atheism, he knew how to handle his stuff, how to get it across . . . Until, having evolved
the first two verses, doubt clouded his satisfaction: "Have
I made myself clear, I wonder?" (Browning did not often
ask himself just that) and he went on to search for an analogy to repeat his meaning on a different slant. And so we
get the vivid image of a shining eagle-feather dropped on
to a moor, which for this had for ever sunk its character
as a moor existing in its own right.

As I remarked before, I too am a hero-worshipper: had
I been living in the eighteen-seventies, after Browning
settled in London, I might have begged him for a contribution to the symposium: "Is hero-worship good for the
soul?" But what's the use? He died in 1889 and I was born
in 1890.

—Good for the soul. Is it also good for biography? Perhaps. We only really worship one or two or at the most three heroes in a lifetime, but nevertheless I hold no brief for the disrespectful biographer. As setting forth the perils of approaching our subject too confidently and with a pre-conceived notion of what we are going to find when we get there, I shall present a pretty little case of how, many years ago, on the one occasion that I met Barrie plain, I also met my come-uppance.

It happened when he was chairman at a dinner given by the Dramatists' Club; and his air of deprecation when he sprang—no, hesitated to his feet to make a speech, his total deficiency in what stage directors call "attack," reminded me of how a cynical contemporary had said of him that "he backed nervously into the limelight." It was an excellent speech; but in my undiscriminating phase of literary "realism" I could not see the genius in his plays because of all the whimsical tricks and fancies with which he chose to obscure it; so that after dinner, finding myself entangled in a little group where the conversation (I forget how or why) had turned on to the jargon of cryptic signs, I thought I would draw him out into a typical Barrie-ism— Heaven forgive my arrogance!—and mentioned that when I was a child I had always wondered over a capital H, blue on a white ground, displayed over and over again on London railings or on the wall of a house—"I still don't know what it means?" He, however, refusing to avail himself of the cutest, quaintest little doorway that ever swung open into a Never-Never-Land or an Island that Likes to be Visited or a Wood of Second Chances on Midsummer Eve, merely replied, blunt and informative: "Oh, that just means hydrant!"

Perhaps the tendency nowadays is to laud austerity beyond its merits. Although there exists a Modern School

which reacts gloomily to happy endings, scornfully dis-
missing them as dope, even they might find austerity un-
desirable where, for instance, apple-trees should be in blossom or raspberry canes in fruit. As for charm—what is it?
The question must remain purely rhetorical; charm need
not be bogus nor facetious; in fact, *real* charm never is,
although one snigger must make it instantly unacceptable.
Bogus charm, winsomely seeking to entangle our affec-
tions by pretending to be as children in a grown-up world,
sends us running harder than we know we had it in us to
run, only so that we should escape. But real charm reveals
the grown-up world through the eyes of a child, and without any pretending.

(And the letter H, affixed to railings or the wall of a
house, just stands for hydrant.)

For Barrie knew when not to tamper with the truth;
but knew also, in spite of Flaubert's rule "there is a certain
unknown quantity in the smallest thing; find it," that there
is sometimes a delicate relish in not being told the whole
truth. One might have a rough shot at it, just to oblige
magistrate or judge. But the *whole* truth would need to be
drawn up from the bottom of the bottomless well by a
bucket with a hole in it. We have only to consider the
comic dissimilarity of a man's autobiography and his biography, to become aware that truth has fantastically little
to do with what people believe about themselves and what
other people believe about them. A sort of general resemblance may emerge; biography and autobiography about
to pass one another in the street . . . pausing with a puzzled: "Surely we've met before?" Exposed to all the haz-
ards of illusion and disillusion, mistaken certainties and
hopeful optimism, at an arbitrary point of cleavage between being and reporting, during life or after death, these

verdicts get written down, and at intervals down the years reconsidered and rewritten, and still (as we say of a jelly) they cannot be said to have "set" into the truth and *nothing* but the truth. Especially difficult the question of nothing but the truth. What, stick to the point? No digressions? Forego every delicious inconsequent that-reminds-me? "Tell us the simple facts, there's no need for more," an encouraging voice addresses the witness-box. Yet almost at once superfluous festoons begin to hang round the edge of the simple facts; that is, if we can manage not to confound "simple" with its direct opposite, shallow. "What is truth? said jesting Pilate"—though of course he was never further from jesting on the most agonizing dilemma that ever in the history of the world dug horns into a well-meaning, ineffective Proconsul of Rome.

For a professional story-teller who starts to plan his autobiography, it is hard to discriminate between the truth of what we remember, and the dreamy never-ending flow of what we think we remember. As for successful biography, when all the necessary research has been done, all contributions gathered in, still there must remain a mysterious gift which perhaps we can compare with the water-diviner's uncanny faculty as he passes the hazel twig over the ground selected for experiment, to feel it of its own volition lift and leap. Facts and observation can never be enough for biography, nor an alliance of lucky opportunity and conscientious labor; never can the twig lift without that quality we call evocation.

As a title least evocative of the treasure we are to find within, I should choose *Performing Flea*, by which P. G. Wodehouse very nearly damned his autobiography before we even got past the dust-jacket. A Wodehouse fan, I am compelled to admonish him, gently flicking a cane: "Come, come, my boy, modesty is all very well, but you can do better than this!"—holding up as examples of what could be achieved in titles for an autobiography, Angela du Maurier's ironic *It's Only the Sister*, probably a lifetime of rueful acceptance packed into one brief, easily remembered phrase; or Noel Coward's well-tailored *Present Indicative*; or that sad, most significant title to all our autobiographies, first discovered by A. A. Milne: *It's Too Late Now*.

A subtle smile may occasionally hover at the corner of my lips; but Mr. Wodehouse alone among our living humorists of stage and pen can cause me over and over again to become a veritable laughing jackass. So that when I met him in person—(like Barrie, only once)—and finding myself placed beside him at dinner, it was all I could do to control a spate of rapturous gratitude, remembering that spates can prove embarrassing and that it is only the Second-class Great who welcome them. "Mr. Wodehouse," I longed to say, "never mind about being politely concerned because nobody has passed me the *aubergines farcies*; much as I appreciate them, I would rather babble appreciation of the Wodehouse idiomatic dialogue, so easy until somebody else tries to copy it; that ingenious Wodehouse plot showing us a good man beset by circumstances over which he has no control, yet agile at evading them as a long-limbed Harlequin who can fling sausages gaily with the Clown and hit the Policeman every time—" At this point he asked me, his mild blue gaze limpid and sincere: "Do tell me, *how* do you get your plots? I'm so bad at finding plots." And afterwards I learned that he had said to our hostess, "Do you think she'll *mind* if I talk to her about her books?" What, *mind?* Me mind if the man whom Hilaire Belloc twice publicly acknowledged as "the finest living writer of English prose" asked me anything, ever? His habit, while he lived in London, of throwing stamped and addressed letters out of the window of the fourth-floor flat, for any passer-by to pick up and deliver (because he said in that fashion they reached their destination far quicker than if he posted them in the conventional way) either reveals a childlike innocence and a readiness to be exploited, which is plain idiotic, or on the other hand touches an apotheosis of worldly nonchalance which few of us can emulate. Such unconscious revelation in autobiography is eventually far more valuable than all the factual knowledge assembled by the biographer's industry and skill; factual knowledge may get in the way, like tables and chairs, china cabinets and tallboys, screens and footstools, in an over-furnished room; the enthusiastic biographer must learn not to get in the way of his subject— and indeed, an even harder lesson, so must the diffident autobiographer.

I once flippantly put forth a project of writing Barrie's life in the form of fiction, Chapter I beginning: "This puir motherless bairn . . ." And after that, nobody could possibly have guessed whom I meant. But then, as already related, our one meeting cramped my style and taught me humility. "I have always thought that I was rather realistic," protested Barrie to the Critic's Circle. No, he was never "*rather* realistic"; never watered down his cold, bitter realism to a *rather*; preferring more often than not, to switch over to whimsy unashamed. Yet what exactly *is* whimsy? "It is, I suppose, an attempt to catch people's sentiments with the bribe of false coin; a sort of charlatanry"—I came across the definition in the pre-

face to a collection of Barrie's speeches published in 1938;
and interested to see who had had courage, furthermore,
to laud Barrie (of all people) for "discipline and econ-
omy" in his writing, I turned to the title page; interest
did not abate on the discovery that it was Hugh Walpole; his definition of whimsy could be bracketed with
Clifford Bax's equally lucid pinning-down of sentimentality as "a word which ought to mean spilling emotion beyond the receptivity of the subject." Not that Hugh
Walpole was a genius like Barrie, but it was salutary to
find an author who was himself to be victim of post-
mortem belittlement—(despite Rupert Hart-Davis's excellent and unprejudiced biography)—employing exactly
the right words for that better half of Barrie which was
so definitely not McConnachie; the half that he teasingly
chose to deny by lethal tricks and devices which a quarter
of a century ago Evelyn Waugh taught us to reject in
the phrase "too too sick-making." Lady Cynthia Asquith,
who had not my advantage of having only met him once,
but for twenty years functioned as personal secretary to
this impish, weary, fierce, sarcastic, provocative, disconcerting, kindly little man, the Biographer's Headache, the
Psycho-analyst's Whiteheaded Boy, her *familiar* in the
most affectionate sense of a term usually abused by war-
lock connections, contrived nevertheless to keep him this
side idolatry with only infrequent excursions across the
borderline. And such privileged intimacy has enabled her
to assist in the disposal of the Great Barrie Fallacy, that
he was himself The Boy Who Wouldn't Grow Up; to
her it was pitifully plain that truth lay in a reversal of
the verdict; the creator of Peter Pan, she said, had been
a case not of arrested but of precipitated development, a
man who had had to grow up much too soon, conjecture

which has undoubtedly rung the tinker-bell. Her authority supports a theory I have always held, that Master Jamie
could have stopped all his whimsy at any moment if he had
wanted to; the mystery and puzzle of his gnome-like
genius lay in his *not* wanting to: anyhow, not often
enough. Yet *Mary Rose* and *Dear Brutus*, sardonically
down to bedrock in their conclusions, are in danger of
being overlooked when posterity hands out its Oscars,
because they have naturally been printed to include his
full stage directions, about half a page of them to a one-
line speech. Try crossing them out—(always fun to cross
out other writers' superfluities in that dashing style!)—
and see what magnificent bone-structure is left bare.

Our more adult neighbors on the continent, confirm-
ing Kipling's impatient dictum that "Allah created the
English mad, the maddest of all mankind," are inclined
to wonder at the national infantilism which slants a light
on our stubborn adhesion to the annual revival of the play,
now past its half-centenary; on Peter Pan's fundamental
unwillingness to renounce childhood; a trait chiefly to be
found in England and America where "he's just a boy at
heart" is always spoken with an indulgent, not an exas-
perated inflection; it is clear, however, that no irresponsi-
ble Peter Pan could have been responsible for the creation of Peter Pan; and a provocative discovery, by Roger
Lancelyn Green, of Barrie's hitherto unpublished *Scenario
for a Proposed Film of Peter Pan*, gives us a chance to
marvel at the difference, comparing it with the stage
directions in his published plays, directions often arch
enough to make a strong man squirm in agony; while in
most of his film scenario, the wording is terse, practical,
and completely down to earth.

Let me here add an item of personal testimony to the

potency of Barrie magic; in 1944 a couple of Guards officers, tall and splendid, dropped in to see *Peter Pan* during their last leave before being sent abroad; remarking in lordly fashion that they might as well, they hadn't seen it since they were kids. Presently they began to cry . . . and went on weeping uncontrollably all through the play, so they told me; stared at with profound interest by a throng of children around them in the stalls; one small inquisitor apparently twisted round in his seat and knelt with his back to the stage in order to miss nothing of a better show. The subsequent gallant behavior of both officers on the field of battle naturally bore no relation whatsoever to their odd break-down when confronted with a strange boy flying in through the window of the Darlings' night-nursery. . . .

Autobiography spilling itself into a pretense of fiction is the writer's own business; and when Barrie has shed the handicap of "I" and "me," we learn more about him from the ironic realism of the Kirriemuir novels, *Sentimental Tommy* and *Tommy and Grizel*, than from his deliberate self-exposures, skilfully edited, in *My Lady Nicotine, A Window in Thrums* and worst of all *Margaret Ogilvie*. Worst? It depends whether or not one is profoundly thankful that Elizabeth Barrett Browning, with every capacity for illusion about her Daddy, never handed them down to us. Miss Mitford did, we know, illusions and all. And Louisa May Alcott, in sundry battered volumes on our nursery bookshelves, *Little Women, Good Wives, Little Men* and *Jo's Boys*, where Bronson Alcott's daughter took us on a personally conducted tour through those nebulous regions that twist between fact and fiction. Unlike most children's stories of the same period, these grow old but never old-fashioned, so that when we grow old ourselves (but, let us pray, never old-fashioned) and read as though in a puzzled dream a sober biography of Louisa Alcott, the chapters alternately serve or snub our memories; because Louisa's protective instinct, functioning like mad, indulges her father-fixation by portraying "Mr. March" as "Jo" saw him; whereas it had no need to protect "Marmee," nor her sisters "Meg," "Beth," and "Amy" (Annie, Lizzie and May). For just this beloved father was the snag in the Alcott family life—may Louisa forgive me for putting it so disrespectfully!—and the cause of a hundred painful episodes which had to be manipulated to make a plausible figure, wise, brave and unselfish; as an instance, in truth it was Louisa, not her father, who could not endure to remain passive during the Civil War, but had to go off and nurse the wounded in the Union Hospital at Georgetown. A shock too, for readers of *Little Women*, to find that the popular character of "Laurie" had never existed in the flesh except as two separate boy companions cleverly blended, Alf Whitman and Ladislas Winiewski; while bushy beaming Professor Bhaer was part invention and partly suitor and husband not to "Jo" but to the youngest sister May whom in *Good Wives* Louisa chose to mate with "Laurie." Louisa did not marry anyone; her stalwart generous nature presented her instead with as many chances as a quick-change artist could desire of being husband, daughter, mother, father, sister, aunt and godmother to the troubles of the entire Alcott family; they were her true career, always to take precedence of that small matter of achieving a book for juveniles, which still touches America to the same pride as Denmark has in Hans Andersen, and we in our own Lewis Carroll.

She was a born hero-worshipper; Dickens had been her

far-off idol, but once she saw and heard him perform at his famous reading-desk, she suffered a bitter disappointment. Fortunately—or do I mean unfortunately?—her illusions about Bronson Alcott were never destroyed, and nor indeed were his in the same comfortable direction; he remained complacently unaware that his family were victims of an unpractical ideology; and they continued to adore him and to make the best of existence up and down the hearbreak scale of unjustified optimism and desperate poverty. For many years, whatever Louisa earned by her scribbling (according to a clever summing-up in Madeleine Stern's biography) she "invested in the Alcott sinking fund, the Micawber Railroad, and the Skimpole three per cents." Not too inadequately he wrote in a Sonnet to Louisa: "I press thee to my heart as Duty's faithful child." How characteristic, then, that she should have "caught her death," as the phrase goes, still and gladly making a burnt-offering of Bronson Alcott's daughter to Bronson Alcott; she was fifty-six when, during one of her too frequent periods of illness, she went to him as he lay dying, and outlived him by only six days.

Presenting truth in the form of fiction is a tricky business; the writer's more usual job consists in making fiction seem like truth. Though of course it is difficult for us who have not delved deep into research, to judge exactly where fact does fringe off into story. When impartial biographers choose to let truth masquerade as fiction, there are rules which have to be observed; or let us say one inflexible rule: they are allowed to fill in blank spaces with fabrication (as long as this remains in character) but never never tamper with known facts. A paucity of surviving facts can be a help: when Gerald Bullett wrote *The Alderman's Son* in the guise of a novel about a boy in Warwickshire, Will Shaxper, his family and his school-days, so little was positively known of Shakespeare's early life that his author-biographer could allow imagination free pasture for its roaming and still not violate the rule nor destroy the appearance of authenticity.

Can "remembering" be fairly listed under autobiography? Yes, if the writer's memory does more than just hang about whimpering on the threshold of *temps perdu*. Marcel Proust must be awarded the title of Lord High Rememberer for all countries and all times. In a long series of autobiographical novels he reveals such a magical gift for "revisiting" the period of his past, that no competitors of our own country, we may be sure, would ever dream of calling themselves competitors at all, but acknowledge Proust as *hors de concours*. Yet while leaving the front row uncontested to this solitary occupant, it seems to suit the English temperament to write with a pretense of invention to cover self-consciousness, as though a cloak were loosely draped over their shoulders. Recently just such a "novel" appeared, joyously headed for the kingdom of minor classics; so far we have had no proof that *Morning* by Julian Fane is a vivid portrayal of Julian Fane's own boyhood—"But of course it *is*," we remark confidently; "it must be!" Two other of our professional rememberers, Compton Mackenzie and Jocelyn Brooke, both in admirable control of afterthought and delusion, reject the Proustian technique of bringing out novel after novel with "moi" as a fictional character; Jocelyn Brooke in *Private View* has no objection to featuring as the little boy he has once been, and then let his mature mind comment on these childish impressions of people and places and exciting events; as when he was allowed to Have the Magic Lantern, a quaint, cumbersome ritual comparing

quaintly with the slick screen magic of films and tele-
vison which the modern child takes for granted. He has
a somewhat wry quality altogether missing from Compton Mackenzie's memories of early childhood appearing
either as fiction in *Sinister Street*, or in their own right
in a later volume called *Echoes*. Compton Mackenzie does
not wallow in the seas washing round the Isles of Nostalgia, he dives briskly in, and then swims vigorously back
to land to display his booty. And we accept with awe
his statement that, except once for a very short period,
he never kept a diary; remembering for him is indeed
remembering and not consulting notes on that bountiful
era which included horse omnibuses and Drury Lane
pantomimes; the summer smell of water-carts laying the
dust in the quiet streets of West Kensington; a carriage
and pair drawn up in the Hammersmith Road with a
Victorian old lady in a mushroom hat—more than Victorian, Queen Victoria herself—bowing to him repeatedly
from the landau; and a schoolboy at Colet Court making
lofty references to "my kiddie sister." His portraits of the
Great are drawn with infectious chuckles and a keen
sense of the ridiculous. At my two or three meetings with
Sir Compton during the past ten years, he has rendered
such a superb performance of what in other men must
remain anecdotes, that I am constantly reminded that he
comes of a great acting family—"my kiddie sister" is Fay
Compton—and that two careers are still open to him with
equal certainty of fame in either.

The five volumes of Osbert Sitwell's autobiography
form a chronicle built in splendid terraces, where the
pageant he musters by his special gift as literature's Earl
Marshal, parades for our entertainment; using his phenomenal powers of memory before two world wars, but

in gratitude for the world we have had, instead of in short, sharp, irritated barks of resentment at the world we have got. One reason for his success may be that he never writes on a subject where he is not reassuringly at home and in his element. " 'E dunno where'e are" is a reproach that can never be levelled at Sir Osbert: wherever 'e is, 'e knows where 'e are. Especially in *Great Morning*, where every incident proves exciting and significant: if he happens to catch a cold in the head, they put him to bed in the Tower of London where his battalion was attached; and in his vision of the Tower, magic and romance live by a lyric beauty of phrase that transcends even the golden descriptions of his beloved Renishaw, or of the vast city within a castle in Italy, a dwelling roomy enough for three hundred people, bought by his father as a desirable bijou residence and a shining example to his family not to be extravagant ... *Daddy, a Study in Survival* portrayed with that touch of genius we associate with famous Victorian parenthood translated into fiction: Mr. Micawber and Mr. Pontifex and the Great Mel, who were Dickens's father and Samuel Butler's and George Meredith's. Sir George Sitwell's theory of educating his elder son, it would seem, was to discover what he enjoyed doing, and instantly stop him from doing it; his idea of pampering, to bestow on him in early manhood a shilling a week pocket-money, and then ask him how he wasted it? It should be a matter of just pride for the author that his acceptance of outrageous tyranny never loses proportion and becomes personally bitter and reproachful. Sir George always pointed to himself—(sincerely, one is led to believe)—as a model of austerity and self-sacrifice, while he never ceased from complicated schemes of expenditure: " 'What we want there is just a cascade betweeen the distant trees. Nothing looks so well or points a view so aptly as falling water! Not everyone can manage it—but it's quite easy for me.' And added confidentially, with a little smile of self-congratulation, 'Between ourselves, I have over two miles of lead-piping up my sleeve!' "

His domestic outlook was Pond Life at its simplest, blind to any form of existence except his own: "It was plain to him," remarked Osbert, admirably detached, "that the less you knew people, and the shorter the time you had known them, the less likely they were to contradict you." Irony has worked it out as a joke in the best possible taste that he should have been lifted high among the Comic Immortals; lifted by that very son whom once he hauled out of the Guards to come home and painfully acquire a decent handwriting by practicing pothooks, so that at least he might earn a bare living as a clerk.

It must be plain by now that I fell headlong in love with Sir George.

Conscious of having been one of the lucky few in a doomed generation, Osbert Sitwell's outburst of loyal rage on behalf of the young men, his friends, who were destroyed by the war of 1914, recalls the mood of Zola's *J'Accuse*, and recently of *Look Back in Anger*, accusing something, someone, of not caring enough! The final chapters of *Great Morning*, my own special award of an O. M. among the four volumes of his autobiography, gather to a crescendo of brilliant living in that enchanted age just before August 1914; a swelling hymn of praise; then a sorrowful drop . . . Ichabod, the glory is departed.

"It's a fair Itchabod, old man. There's no going back to things like that."—This was no longer Osbert Sitwell, but H. G. Wells's little drapery apprentice, Mr. Polly; and his was a poor morning. Yet if we view them both as auto-

biography and equally true as the social history of two
human beings living through much the same period, it
hardly matters that one of our heroes develops as himself, and the other becomes representative of a million
other Mr. Pollys who were offered up body and soul
to a system of education—

> "which left his mind . . . in much the same state that you
> would be in . . . if you were operated upon for ap-
> pendicitis by a rather well-meaning, boldly enterpris-
> ing, but rather overworked and underpaid butcher
> boy, who was superseded towards the climax of the
> operation by a left-handed clerk of high principles
> but intemperate habits"—

victim of a father who totally disregarded an idea deep
in his son's being that "somewhere were pure and easy
and joyous states of body and mind," but merely remarked "It's time that dratted boy did something for a
living"; and in the exact arbitrary spirit of Sir George
Sitwell, put him to serve in a drapery store.

H. G. Wells was my first literary hero to stop and speak
to me and let me speak to him again, often and often, but
chiefly during the span of years stretching from 1915 to
1939. He died in 1946. And I think he would have been
glad to know how his ghost would feel to me—"just mel-
lowish and warmish like," as he had prophesied, Mr. Polly
as his mouthpiece; Mr. Polly seated on a bench outside
the Potwell Inn quietly watching the sunset:

> "Come here always, when I'm a ghost."
> "Spoil the place for others," said the fat woman.
> "Not my sort of ghost wouldn't," said Mr. Polly . . .
> "I'd be a sort of diaphalous feeling—just mellowish
> and warmish like. . . ."

Wells and Priestley and Aldous Huxley have one major preoccupation: the obstinacy by which men all the time persist in retaining unhappiness in their lives, and how can an author, made responsible by seeing what is going on, wake them from their bad dream except perhaps by use of their own experiences on this perplexing problem? Wells chose to do it via fiction, leaving us to extract the autobiography for ourselves; *Love and Mr. Lewisham*, *Kipps*, *Mr. Polly*, *Tono Bungay*, and *Mr. Britling sees it through*, leave us provided with everything except mystery; H. G. had no use for human mystery; scientific mysteries, yes; they were different, and maybe when he first conceived *The Time Machine* or *The Food of the Gods* they were an escape from that constant girding at an impersonal problem in his case so intensely personal: why *can't* men—? why *don't* men—? what *makes* men—? and oh dear, oh dear, *must* they go on wearing boots that hurt their feet? Foolish, lovable, semi-ignorant little men! Obstinate, blind, muddled little men . . . trying their best.

J. B. Priestley has also frequently tried to worry it out on behalf of this stubborn generation; sometimes in autobiography: *Midnight in the Desert*, *Rain over Gadshill*, and a most delectable volume, *Delight*; and sometimes again in his plays. It may be that though he has never conceived an immortal Kipps or Mr. Polly, he comes nearer than H. G. to expressing what the common man lacks of delight, and something more of why he so unhappily misses it. "Seek ye first the Kingdom of God . . ." It was fun, at the end of the first night of *Johnson over Jordan*, to hear the audience, as they trooped out, speculating as to what the dramatist *meant* by the tremendous implication in that last quiet curtain? They might have been more justified in their bewilderment over his plays that adapt Ratty's discovery in *The Wind in the Willows*: "There is *nothing*—absolutely nothing— half so much worth doing as simply messing about in boats" . . . "as simply messing about in Time" says Mr. Priestley. Not that I could bear to forfeit Time's peculiar palindrome on which he shaped *I Have Been Here Before* for any steadier sequence of yesterday leading us through today into tomorrow—"and straight on till morning."

I had an impression of Aldous Huxley among those who only once stopped and spoke to me. But memory, stumbling back the other day into a *recherche du temps perdu*, found evidence of a second encounter in the early 1930's, at lunch in the garden of an *auberge* somewhere along the coast of the Mediterranean; for I had had the sense to scribble down a few rough notes when I got home, intending them ultimately to form part of a biographical essay which should have the gloss and smoothness of polished ivory . . . but you know what it is!

At this lunch my normal faculties were subdued in the company of a brain great enough to put all ours out of action; yet not too subdued for silent amusement at noticing how if one of the party brought up a topic with any personal implication, Huxley immediately cut the umbilical cord and let it loose again. Provided a subject could be kept impersonal, however, he went into it with mathematical accuracy and precision. What a contrast with nearly all of us who sometimes subtly and sometimes by methods painfully obvious, attempt to work round from the general to the particular; but directly this happened in Huxley's presence, he stopped talking, lowered his head, and removed himself from contemporary life until we had ceased to be so distressingly *local*. Thus I doubt if he could have told what I looked like, but I retain a

clear picture of him: the strange dilation of his eyes owing
to powerful lenses; the pale face and thick untidy dark
hair and lovely hands with long eloquent fingers. Wearing a huge sombrero, thin open shirt and slacks, all white
—laboratory white not beachcomber white (the difference
between dazzling and dirty, in the South of France)—
he arrived at the *auberge*, sat down at the table, and did
not utter for at least ten minutes; had I been his mother
I would have said: "Don't put your face down in the
plate, dear, it's not very polite; here's kind Miss Stern who
has come all this way to see you." Then suddenly everything was all right—more than all right, "memorabilia"!
A strange collection went into these notes that I have not
looked at for twenty-five years: Maharajahs, for instance,
and the jewels they wear, and the synthetic making of
jewels; some mosaics discovered at Damascus; and curing leather in Mexico—and here I had to pore over two
words inserted in the margin: "horses' excrement"; allusion which might have referred to its use for curing
leather in Mexico, or might equally have been some fascinating observation that had no connection with leather
—I ought to have enlarged on it or left it out altogether
from my notes. Then came a lament for the flower-fields
round Grasse: how dreadful that scent could be got out
of *coal*; a factory at Chesterfield . . .

Wait a moment; here, after all, is a scrap of personal
autobiography that must have slipped past his sentries: a
remark that he hated writing, and loved painting in oils.
Painting, he said, was "using your hands mentally," and
he enjoyed seeing his thoughts come out in physical substance—"*lumps* of oil" exclaimed Aldous Huxley with peculiar relish. Abnormally short-sighted, he had to paint
everything at close range. Once he actually succeeded in

"catching a likeness," though he did not say of whom. Flippantly I suggested an idea for a story in which all the authors of the world threw up writing and took to painting instead; he took this quite seriously; thought it more than probable that they might, because writers frequently turn to painting, but painters rarely if ever become writers.

Suddenly seized with a passionate desire to discover the germ and reason for best-sellerdom, he sought to work it down to some tiny first cause as, for instance, the weather? "Take Florence Barclay"—(the command was purely rhetorical)—"she always wrote about elderly and ugly women married to very young men who went blind; now why should that have sent her sales rocketing up into tens of thousands?" (Always? Well, once; but there was more value in a Huxley monologue than in logical argument, so I kept silent and listened.) "And take Sherlock Holmes! How stimulating in that Victorian era of high morality, that the hero of popular stories could be a dope fiend and get away with it! Give me Ouida!—" (again the demand was rhetorical)—"But why, on the other hand, should a book containing none of the best-seller ingredients, not sacrifice nor sadism, still attain such startling success as the *Outline of Philosophy?* Now the Fabulists knew their way to the place where we kept our wishful thinking and made a bee-line for it: reassure your readers and they'll remain your readers for the next twenty years."

Then he made a joke, that the situation in India (I forget what was then "the situation in India") was probably due to his lowering British prestige by having no white tie with him when he went out there; a joke too "petite" for Aldous Huxley; a little-man-joke, cherubic, chirping . . .

it was difficult for us to know what to do with a joke on such a small scale; had his treatise on mescalin already appeared, I might have carried on the mood with something idiotic about his infatuation, when under the influence of the drug, with the flowing beauty of the creases in his trousers. But mescalin still lay twenty years ahead of our lunch in the dancing heat of June on the shores of the Mediterranean; a lunch that as far as I was concerned, could have gone on for ever, because in a strange way I was enchanted. In the genial company of H. G. Wells you could be conscious of a home from home; and when he ragged you, rag him back again, remind him of his naughty fit of temper when he lost at ping-pong and cast his bat to the floor . . . But to rag the author-to-be of *Grey Eminence* was unthinkable. Not that he was stiff; not that he was formal; not that he lacked simplicity; indeed, if someone were shy and not at ease, you felt he might wonder "What have I done?" or even "How can I put this right?" modestly setting it down to any cause under the sun, in fact, except "I am Aldous Huxley."

Our first meeting was also in the South of France, at a villa I had rented at Anthéor where the rocks were red. The program of our days, if it included a couple of hours glorious bathing from the rock island before lunch and then an abundance of *vin du pays*, naturally required a siesta after lunch. All the doors of the villa led into the central *salon*; and behind every door, the strong light filtering through drawn green *jalousies*, lay a naked body on the bed, happy, exhausted, replete, stupefied with sun and sea and salt. Suddenly came a knock at my door; modesty caught up a wrap, flung it round and went crossly to see who it was. There stood John van Druten, struck all of a heap . . . Reverently he intoned, long pauses between each word: "Aldous—Huxley—is—in—the—garden!"

Brutally cheerful and matter-of-fact, I replied: "Well, be your age, Johnny! Tell him to come in."

It took me a little while to dress, and when I went into the salon, Niki and Freda were volubly entertaining Maria Huxley at one end of the room; Johnny was standing by the window at the other end "entertaining" Eddy Sackville-West (in deathly silence); and quite by himself in the middle of the room, seated uncomfortably on a hard chair at the table, nobody speaking to him, was Aldous Huxley, no doubt moodily wondering why he had come.

That party never really got going; which is why I chose to describe our second meeting first.

Some people might think it was a far cry from Aldous Huxley to Groucho Marx; and yet I don't know—were I to see them photographed arm-in-arm, with the caption "Chums," I might not be unduly astounded; Mr. Huxley will forgive me (or, more likely, will not care a damn one way or the other) if I link them by that very quality of *strangeness*; though the scholar's face, thin and slightly ecclesiastical might not have so startled me as Groucho's when I suddenly caught sight of the latter leering up at me from the top of a pile of volumes in a Catholic bookshop a few days before Christmas, 1955. Groucho's biography, written by his son Arthur, had just been published; after reviewing it with immense relish, I bestowed it (unwrapped) on Pamela Frankau as a somewhat inappropriate Yuletide gift, when we met to buy the right sort of Christmas cards in one of the shops that cluster round Westminster Cathedral. Pamela generously stood me a couple of Catholic books which I took some time to select; and after mooching round a bit, we went into the Cathedral, and in the fullness of time hailed a taxi to go home. Just as we were getting in, I looked at Pamela's armful of parcels and gently asked "Exactly *where*, my darling, did you shed Groucho?"

Slow dawn of horror in her eyes . . . She leapt out, gave the driver my address, and dashed away. Later she rang me up and I heard the story of her vain search, first inside the Cathedral where she most dreaded to see those rolling orbs, that cocked cigar, that wacky grin, obviously making a characteristic wisecrack. Either the Cardinal had strolled in, noticed it, remarked "Hallo, what's this?" and appropriated it for his own recreation, or it was lying incongruous and unabashed among the Three Kings and the Nativities in the Christmas card department of the shop opposite. Hoping yet dreading, she revisited every place where she had lingered to choose, to buy, to pay. Not a sign. At last she gave up and was on the point of departure . . . when she beheld Groucho lying face upwards on top of a pile of books, dominating all the neighboring piles of literature sacred and holy, and somehow managing to make it look as though the whole of the stack underneath him similarly consisted of biographies of Groucho Marx. The crowds passing to and fro, lingering to browse, looked astonished at such a bizarre departure from the traditions of the Catholic Truth Society store. And indeed, it would have required a lot of explanation. Pamela waited until just for a moment she thought nobody was noticing, snatched up her property, and slithered away . . . I thought she sounded much older than when we were together, an hour before.

Young Groucho's biography of his father, written in equal parts of deep affection and devilish acumen, was enlivened by Daddy's frequent footnotes—("*Take it easy*

*with that probing. If I want to be analyzed, I'll go to a
psychiatrist. GROUCHO.*") The private life of this
middle brother of the famous Marx quintet—("four alive
and one in the fur trade," as Groucho once informed me)
—reveals the most unlikely traits. There is a good deal to
be said for biography written by a member of the family,
with all the advantages of inside information. Improbable
as it may seem, Groucho was a steady, reliable fellow;
he preferred going to bed early, and strong drink meant
nothing to him. Especially endearing are those pages deal-
ing with his home life, which according to his son, must
have been "a pretty confusing atmosphere in which to
grow up." Julius ("Groucho") loved being at home. He
"revelled in the disrespect of his children," and nevertheless was almost mid-Victorian in some of his rules, remarkably strict about early bed-time and so forth. When he
played the buffoon in public he liked to combine being
thoroughly obstreperous with retaining a complete ano-
nymity.

I cannot catalogue our friendship under "met him
once"; thrice, perhaps, during my stay in Hollywood;
which would work out roughly the same as twenty times
with a personality less exuberant. At my first encounter in
the winter of 1933, he was lying on a couch beneath a
rose-shaded lamp, having the soles of his feet tickled by
his pretty wife. He explained that his ecstasy was heredi-
tary: "We boys did it for nothing whenever Mother
wanted it, but would you believe it, my children charge
me a dollar an hour!"

Still beguiled by the theme of family biographies which
might have been entitled "Daddy," though I have never
met du Maurier's daughter Daphne who wrote *Gerald*,
I had several meetings with her father; the first in his

dressing-room, when I boldly impersonated an interviewer who had a brief appointment to ask his opinion on
—I forget what—an anthology of Should Someone Do
Something? Presently he discovered that I was an author
in my own right, not an interviewer from Woman's
What-have-you, and asked why I had bothered to come?
"Because I wanted to meet you." "Oh, am I as good as all
that?" "Yes," emphatically. Yes, he was indeed as good
as all that, and my favorite actor for many years. After
his death, I got involved in not a few rumpuses on the
book of *Gerald* with those of his old friends who chose
to consider it disrespectful because his second daughter,
loving him, had a sense of character which would not be
denied; she "saw him plain" and saw him in his home life,
and what emerged clearly was the Peter Pan in him, the
boy who wouldn't grow up, the practical joker; the actor
who had his audiences in tears at that moment in the third
act of *Dear Brutus* when he entered from the Enchanted
Wood and explained that he couldn't stay a moment—
"My daughter's waiting for me . . . my daughter . . ." and
then the stricken look on his face at the gradual realization that she was only a dream-daughter. But when he
went home to three flesh-and-blood girls with claims and
personalities of their own, such evidence of his maturity
filled him with dismay: what did one *do* about real
daughters? A fellow-actor, registering indignation and
loyalty about the book and not pausing to wonder which
side I was on, said: "Why, we were all like schoolboys,
and Gerald was our captain!" "That's just it," I replied
drily. For the gentleman's mistake lay in seeing no difference between debunking your subject, as in the fashion
set by Lytton Strachey, and simply correcting misappre-
hension by telling the truth; debunking takes a mis-

chievous pleasure in exposure for its own sake. Rarely can a biographer survey his subject with the cool and orderly precision of accountancy; Mr. Somerset Maugham said about novelists that they are at the mercy of their bias; and biography likewise is wont to conceal a preference, small but wilful, an invisible pendulum to swing towards this heap of evidence or that ("Codlin's the friend, not Short"); implying no slipshod methods in research, merely that where the matter rests on surmise, our subconscious cleverly allows itself to depend rather on conjectures to its own liking, than on the no less honest opposition; while "the legend goes" is a scornful phrase which can be used with conviction by both sides. That is why a pre-publication announcement *Letters hitherto unpublished* must always add value to a new biography, because in letters a biographer's bias cannot intrude; unless perhaps in the choice of them.

Nevertheless, it is curious that even beyond our subconscious, beyond the author's control, still and always must remain an impulse of pure creation, a super-arithmetic outside all mathematical formulae. Look at the Forsyte Saga, now generally acknowledged as largely based on true family history. Originally Galsworthy meant Irene to conquer all hearts, and Soames Forsyte to be the villain of the saga; yet as the characters developed and grew older, our perverse sympathies tended to glance aside and fix themselves on Soames; until reading of his death in *Swan Song*, there remained no longer any doubt on whose behalf our hearts were broken.

"I was glad I was myself, and that, I think, is the beginning and end of the conscious content people call happiness . . ."

And with my thanks to R. F. Delderfield for the quotation, that, I think, may also be the beginning and end of good autobiography, which must always work out as a thankful autobiography; not from any expedient motive to create pleasant reading, but because evil forgotten and beauty remembered will perforce balance harmoniously. The secret of fair biography may simply be that the writer cannot prevent himself from liking his subject; whereas certain authors on both sides of the Atlantic are apt to treat him as the fore-doomed victim of a blood sport, to be hunted down and brutally mauled, till we begin to wonder if we should not perhaps call in the Royal Society for Prevention of Cruelty to Animals.

Autobiography can hardly be achieved without including an abundance of detail left over from the chronicler's nursery days, when his mother and father, his aunts and uncles, were giant figures to bestow or withhold the gate-money to paradise; unless, but more rarely—(I can only recall Kenneth Grahame's *Dream Days* and *The Golden Age* as examples)—he chooses to view "the grown-ups" from an aloof, slightly scornful vantage, as Olympians who could enjoy themselves with abandon if they willed it, but somehow never did. Contemporaries, sisters and brothers, are a different matter; and a lot of vetting must go on before an elderly author is allowed by them to publish his indiscriminate anecdotes of a period when he had the blessed assurance of being at home in a beneficent world in which "a boy could grow up as slowly as he pleased." Leaping like a chamois from author to author, I am now quoting from *A Victorian Boyhood* by L. E. Jones; no dreamy nostalgic ramble through the dear Long Ago, but (despite its title) a procession of fresh delights, an array of small sunlit activities. This style of autobiography, mocking a conventional "story-book" childhood, employs flippancy as an admirable device whereby the author can keep himself this side of self-pity.

Having then thrown out self-pity, expedience and rancor, what are the essential qualities for autobiography besides gratitude for the very gift of life? A passion for honesty? An astringent sense of humor? A touch of mystery? A genuine affection for our fellow-creatures which can survive whatever they may do to us personally? Affection, not naked need; it is wiser not to need them; anyhow not need them socially; an all-social autobiography can be plain hell, page after page recording fashionable routs, a brilliant galaxy of guests lucky enough to have been invited to the Prince's ball: "Everybody who is anybody—" thus the glossies—"everybody who is anybody was present last night . . ." and so on. But autobiography should hold us by revelation, not by tabulation, or it becomes merely glorified *causerie* for which no equivalent exists in the English language; "talk" is too brusque; people might bid one stop talking, but they would hardly be likely to say "Cease your *causerie*"; every now and then one has to invent a word for sheer usefulness, like the cleaning lady who comes in to "oblige."

"Far-flungery" is such a word; I invented it for my swifter convenience when I wanted to mention those biographies or autobiographies which take us to travel in distant lands: the jungle, the Arctic and Antarctic, the swamps of the Congo basin, the Gobi desert, the islands of the Southern Pacific, the peak of the Andes or the Himalayas; I lit upon *far-flungery* when, reviewing *The Bafut Beagles* by Gerald Durrell, I said that for once I was glad I had not rejected it for the unenterprising reason that the scene was laid in the Cameroons and not in

Brighton. I favor Brighton because my early life was very much bound up with it, and also the air suits me, whereas I have the gravest doubts as to whether I could say the same of the Arctic, the Congo basin, or the Gobi desert; I'm a whale for sea air (I wonder if I mean that literally?) as long as it comes with the sound of waves breaking on a lonely headland, or against rocks, or under my bedroom window at night; and in a different style of scenery and context, when I walk out to the end of a pier, before fiends of hell thought of placing canned music at every few yards to make sure we should hear nothing else; and I could eloquently argue against the dictum of an American writer who let one of her characters say: "I don't care for fresh air myself . . . Everything of importance happens indoors." My conversion to far-flungery by *The Bafut Beagles* I attribute to the fact that I fell passionately in love with the Fon of Bafut, and love can demolish one's usual prejudices by one brief sentence. Also he introduced me to a couple of Brow Leaf Toads nannied by a serious-minded chimpanzee called Pavlova . . . And to think I might have altogether missed these enchanting characters merely because of a misleading title —("Oh bother, *another* of those books about hunting!"). I had been about to fling it aside when it fell open at a picture of Pavlova with one foot resting on a Brow Leaf Toad to keep it from escaping, while she held the other upside down in mid-air and scrubbed its stomach free from the clinging mud: "At least they shan't say that I don't send you out clean, whatever sort of a state you come back in."

Nowadays celebrities can hardly hope to go on nestling under their leaves like modest violets in a shady grove, un-

til they choose to retire into the study and write it all
down at leisure in the twilight of their days. Twilight—
does it exist in this twentieth century when privacy is
riddled with observation holes, radio, press interviews,
flashlight photographs, public appearances, and television
as the latest contribution?—"A man can't call his soul his
own"—well, yes, he can, but only (to mix metaphors) by
the skin of his teeth.

Yet still I believe we are inclined to prefer autobiographies which are truthful but (in the modern idiom)
"unrealistic," proving the author likes the human race
although he does not like its silly face, and reject those
of the School which sets forth with a cudgel to assault
such sense of values as we may have been able to retain . . .
I wish, indeed, there were some technique by which I
could revive and quicken for contemporary service certain assemblies of words that have grown threadbare and
almost meaningless from constant repetition, such as the
one about "Why beholdest thou the mote that is in thy
brother's eye" while forgetting to consider the beam in
our own; and "It is more blessed to give than to receive";
"The spirit indeed is willing, but the flesh is weak"; "He
that is without sin among you, let him first cast a stone";
"Man shall not live by bread alone . . ."; and (author's
choice) "If the salt has lost its savour, wherewith shall it
be salted?" As for "Let us eat and drink, for tomorrow we
die," it is curiously often misquoted with "and be merry"
added to eating and drinking, and the emphasis on the
first half of the axiom, forgetting the second.

Pondering on all this, I found myself, as always, sinning
against that stern and excellent clause to be observed in
the unspoken code of the Royal Society of Biographers:

Never lapse into autobiography; you, as a personal you, do not exist; a rule which seems oddly unable to exert an effective control over my subconscious; every time, professionally speaking, that I cannot at once hit on the right word or phrase or solution to extricate myself from a difficult problem, every time when I am dissatisfied with what I have just written and would rather daydream than get on with it, my pencil wanders round and round, and enslaved by long habit, produces those deeply soothing emanations which modern idiom calls "doodling." Apparently there is not a straight line in my system. Take a look at the jacket of this volume and you will see what you might at first believe to be a preliminary design for a wallpaper. A million designs each as infinitesimally different from the other as fingerprints are different, cover all the margins of all my manuscripts and notebooks. My friends who have caught sight of them, for this do I often deface their blotters at week-ends in the country, tell me that it reveals my subconscious to be in a most irascible state, and that I would do well to show the patterns to a psychoanalyst. Like Timon, I lightly fling at these flatterers the dishwater out of a soup-tureen, but otherwise pay no attention.

Yet there are few delights like the illegitimate pleasure of supplying for a practical purpose what one has not created as part of one's legitimate job ... So when in 1936 my publisher happened to pick up one of these subconscious scrolls and thought it would be fun to use it as the jacket for *Monogram* (my first volume of rag-bag memoirs) I purred at the compliment. Now, some twenty years later, again a publisher believes it would be fun to put a sample of my doodles to the same use. At first I hesitated, bashful at remembering Rule I of the R.S.B.:

you, as a personal you, do not exist; because as though
seeking some conceited relief from obscurity, my own
name recurs in these patterns over and over again: sometimes the signature "Gladys Stern" left over from my
school-days—("Now then, Gladys Stern, if you've nothing better to do than scribble during the algebra lesson—")
but more usually my initials, G.B.S. (firmly mine in spite
of competition!). But if the mind had not this involuntary
bias, and the arbitrary handle put to a "personal you"
were not a matter of the most intense gratification to my
psyche, surely all the letters of the alphabet would have
twisted themselves in, or none of them? The letter "M,"
however, perpetually woven into the warp of this doodle
—or is it the woof?—need not necessarily be traced to a
preoccupation with Myself; "M" also stands for Mother
(says Professor Freud); or for May, my only sister's
name; or perhaps for Max or Maugham or Marx
(Groucho); or for the mixed contents drawn from a certain well in Wonderland, mousetraps and the moon and
memory and muchness.

MAX BEERBOHM

F TWO people can't agree about a third person, the one who likes him is right, always."

And truth flashed like lightning, as it must have flashed throughout the Sermon on the Mount

Yet the man who said this to me, while I reverently handed him his hat and scarf in the hall after a small luncheon-party in Albany, the man who said it quite simply, unaware that it would ever go into inverted commas in my mind or in the pages of a book, was Max Beerbohm, not usually associated with Chapter 5 of St. Matthew's Gospel. Here is the context: the name of a mutual friend, an artist, came up casually in the course of our talk, and Max said something not really unkind but gently disparaging. "Don't you like him?" I asked, surprised. A pause, then one eyebrow quizzically cocked at me: "Does anybody?"

I was younger than I am now, and so I broke into eloquent defense of our friend. Max listened, attentive, a

little amused; he was no interrupter of speeches, as most
of us are. When I had quite finished, he lifted his glass
and invited me to drink to this same George (naturally
a pseudonym; I have never known a George). Later,
helping him on with his overcoat, I said, contrite for my
over-vehemence: "I'm sorry I burst out like that about
George; you must have thought me terribly schoolgirlish.
Probably I'm wrong and you're right." And then Max
reassured me by that remark I have quoted at the beginning of this portrait, drawn from the pure fountain of
Christianity. It might easily have been spoken by G. K.
Chesterton; was there an affinity between these two?
Memory gave a twitch, suggesting I had better do some
research before I answered; I like research provided I can
choose the subject; it makes me feel like a scholar; one
who speaks with authority; good for the jolly old inferiority complex. And here is the happy result, in the
Rede lecture delivered by Max Beerbohm:

"I can, if you will let me, lay claim to one little modest
negative virtue. I have always been free from envy.
In the year 1900 I had been considered a rather clever
and amusing young man, but I felt no pang whatsoever
at finding myself cut out at my own game by a sudden
newcomer named G. K. Chesterton, who was obviously
far more amusing than I, and obviously a man of genius
into the bargain."

And indeed there is a resemblance in style and (as we have
just decided) in religion, though Chesterton, unlike Max,
was already a celebrating Christian before he came into
the Catholic Church, and his declarations were positive
and gaily ferocious; but the breeding and style of religion

is in both; not alone style of writing, but style of mind; the author without apparent effort making his readers feel at ease as though their faith brought out the best in him and his gratitude will never let them feel alone while in his company. Nobody would pretend that the work of Max Beerbohm can be all things to all men; his public might, for instance, be subtly different from the public of P. G. Wodehouse . . . (how happy could I be with either were t'other dear charmer away!).

And I was conscious of another odd link between Max and G.K.C.: the former wrote a collection of perfect parodies, *A Christmas Garland*, divided by only a hair's breadth of malice from their originals; and one was entitled "Some Damnable Errors about Christmas, by G. K. Chesterton." Yet after the preliminary fun and games, one began to notice that something very strange had occurred, impalpably Max had dropped the parody and put on Chesterton in a deeper sense, as though unaware of his surrender to a stronger if temporary influence of mind and spirit; a couple of pages written as though thus he felt himself and thus he would write on the Christmas theme and story:

"I select at random two of the more obvious fallacies that obtain. One is that Christmas should be observed as a time of jubilation. This is (I admit) quite a recent idea. It never entered into the tousled heads of the shepherds by night, when the light of the angel of the Lord shone about them and they arose and went to do homage to the Child. It never entered into the heads of the Three Wise Men. They did not bring their gifts as a joke, but as an awful oblation. It never entered into the heads of the saints and scholars, the poets and painters, of the Middle Ages. Looking back across the years, they saw in that dark and ungarnished manger only a shrinking woman, a brooding man, and a Child born to sorrow. The philomaths of the eighteenth century, looking back, saw nothing at all. It is not the least of the glories of the Victorian Era that it rediscovered Christmas. It is not the least of the mistakes of the Victorian Era that it supposed Christmas to be a feast . . . Christmas comes but once a year. Perhaps it does, according to the calendar—a quaint and interesting compilation, but of little or no practical use to anybody. It is not the calendar, but the Spirit of Man that regulates the recurrence of feasts and fasts. Spiritually, Christmas day recurs exactly seven times a week. When we have frankly acknowledged this, and acted on this, we shall begin to realize the Days' mystical and terrific beauty, For it is only everyday things that reveal themselves to us in all their wonder and their splendour."

Then, with hardly a jolt in the transition, he returned again to parody's mischievous exaggeration of Chesterton's own exaggerations, as foreshadowed in the title.

And while we make these unexpected discoveries of Sermons by Max Beerbohm, I must unashamedly quote from myself in a former volume of reminiscences:

Painfully conscious every day of my behavior falling far short of how I should act in big and little things towards God and my fellow-men, was it of any use at least to *seem* different from what I was inside, while still honestly aware that my mental processes going on behind the mask were self-preoccupied? I set forth all this to John Van Druten last time he was in England,

and added that of course I did not mean that from credit-earning motives one should pretend to be better than one really is, but from loyalty to the standards one is known to have adopted: "You can't call it pharisaical, can you, if one hasn't put on an act only to impress the beholder with one's personal goodness? Because acting that goes on and on for a long time could, don't you think, become less and less acting?"

"Yes, that's the theme of The Happy Hypocrite," John reminded me, a little surprised that I should sound as though I had been the first to plant a flag within five feet of the top of Mount Everest.

I could have slain him—or myself. How could I possibly have forgotten a single word written by Max Beerbohm of all people? And especially how could I have forgotten the famous story of Lord George Hell, and how he feel in love on sight with an innocent little dancer, and knew he would have no chance if this clear-eyed child could see his wicked, lecherous face all puffed and swollen and livid with purple veins, oozing sin and self-indulgence; so to woo her he put on the disguising mask of a beautiful young man, pure and unlined; but at last he loved her so much that he had to confess his hypocrisy and remove the mask . . . and waited for her to shrink back from the hideous reality now confronting her. But she said wondering (for why should he so have maligned himself?)—"My dear love, you are even more beautiful without your mask than when you had it on."

One evening in 1931, Max Beerbohm came to dinner —I am trying to say this casually, but my throb of pride cannot be altogether suppressed; lacking it, I should have

been a clod. I had invited Clemence Dane to meet him
because she had just finished adapting *The Happy Hypocrite* for a stage production; he had heartily approved of
the script, but they did not yet know each other. In the
course of a talk on casting, he remarked with an air of
mild surprise, taking ours for granted, that his niece, Viola
Tree, had suggested Ivor Novello (of all actors) for the
part of Lord George Hell, a part undoubtedly to be the
high award of the theatrical season. Suddenly I remembered Ivor's performance as an elderly rheumatic colonel
in the prologue of one of his own plays.

"*Yes,*" I exclaimed, backing Viola Tree with all my
might. And "*Yes,*" cried Clemence Dane.

Max did not exactly use the phrase "Well, seeing as how
you say so," but he did indicate that as three not unintel-
ligent women were all spontaneously in accord, there must
be something in it. And he said I might have the fun of
ringing up Ivor the next morning to tell him. Perhaps I
had angled for this by wishing I could be present when
they gave him the part; a pleasure not to be bought with
money is the pleasure of breaking good news; a pendant
to Cleopatra's easily understandable desire to kill the mes-
senger who brought bad news—(never accept that assignment if you can possibly get out of it!).

"Hullo, Ivor!"

"*Darling—*" etc., etc.

"Ivor"—interrupting his normal exuberance, and making my voice as off-hand as possible—"last night, Max
Beerbohm and Clemence Dane were dining with me here,
and they said"—pause—"they said—we were talking about
the Hypocrite, of course—and they said that **you** were
to be given the part of Lord George Hell."

Thereupon came a long long silence. And at last Ivor's voice in an incredulous whisper:

"*It—isn't—true!*"

Shortly after the crisis which found a questionable respite at Munich, I gave a dinner-party for sixty-four people; no, not in my own dining-room, of course; in a private room at Quaglino's restaurant. This is where I cannot resist looking out the menu, signed by forty-nine out of the sixty-four; and a treasure associated with that evening of October 10th, 1938, from my collection of treasures lovingly hoarded in a casket—well, in an old walnut knife-box: a card from Max, already stamped and written with his name and address to give me no trouble whatever in returning it; and a bewitching little illustration of a white tie and a black tie, for me to put a mark against one and cross out the other, to guide his choice of wear at the forthcoming party.

Naturally I replied: "If you think I'm going to send back an original drawing by Max Beerbohm, you've got another think coming. White tie."

Dementia set in during the period of gestation after the invitation had gone out and the enthusiastic acceptances, conditional acceptances, and tentative semi-refusals—("Unless after all we're back by then")—had come; when I drew chart after chart of tables for six or eight, in the effort to arrange who could be placed next to who without sulks or bloodshed; separating husbands and wives; trying to remember all the famous literary quarrels of the past decade; cancelling it and beginning again every morning when the post came in; and doing my best to appease those disappointed nine or ten males who had

clamored to be put beside Elinor Glyn, then in her beautiful and inscrutable seventies. My final version (almost
life-size) I submitted to Somerset Maugham for his O.K.
After careful scrutiny: "Peter dear, forgive me for saying so, but you've put all your plums at one table." Yes
of course I had; *my* table; I like plums, if they be ripe
enough; H. G. Wells, Somerset Maugham, J. B. Priestley,
Rose Macaulay, and on my right Max Beerbohm; what
was wrong with that? But Great White Chief told me
they had better be distributed over a wider area: "Give
me a difficult table if you like, and I'll look after it for
you." I could conceive few handsomer offers, for he has
no philosophy to endure boredom—and no sense of proportion; if at a safe distance one watches his face at any
dinner-party where he may be bored by his neighbors,
one can see him sink full fathom five, and visibly begin to
die. To encourage him therefore in selfless behavior,
I fixed up a charming table for him to preside over, with
Humbert Wolfe, a fine poet and in his off-time a witty
and agreeable rattle, as assistant producer.

Before we started dinner, when the lions were amicably
roaring over their cocktails, a reporter approached me
("approached" is, I think, the word) and asked for a
line on the original purpose of the party? He must have
been reading *Alice*!—("If a fish came to me, and told me
he was going on a journey, I should say, 'With what
porpoise?'"). When he asked me this, I was stumped; to
him, a party without a porpoise was obviously incredible;
I might have replied with as much cause as the Duchess
of Richmond: "Because I've a presentiment that the Battle of Waterloo is going to be fought tomorrow." My
actual reasons were too cloudy for publicity: I had been
hospitably entertained for years without giving adequate

return, and was taught from early childhood the ancient and honorable sport of flinging back the cutlet; also I prefer my parties to consist of not more than four, but where needs must, not less than sixty-four and be done with it. "Couldn't you just say," I faltered, "that I wanted to see my friends?" The reporter eyed me as though I were feeble-minded, as indeed I was at that moment. "Perhaps," he suggested, "you're giving this party to celebrate the Peace?" Immediately I picked up my little hatchet and cut him down like a cherry-tree. "Well," helplessly, "then what *am* I to say?" I glanced round for inspiration, and caught sight of a cherub face, round blue eyes with up-curling lashes, a wise forehead and childlike smile; refreshed, I turned triumphantly to the reporter: "You may state," firmly, "that I have given this party in honor of Max Beerbohm's return from Italy, to live in England."

> They were men and women. They have
> gone their ways now,
> As men and women must. The high song
> is over.

Many years later, picking up that menu of my eve-of-Waterloo dinner-party, I was chanting a mournful threnody from Humbert Wolfe's Requiem; counting up those who had been present who were now dead—"fourteen out of the sixty-four!" But after giving the matter his statistical consideration, John van Druten said, always inclined to come down firmly on the literal side: "I don't call that many. You've got fifty left."

Anyhow, we were only four for dinner in my own home when I opened for Max a bottle of the famous Steinberg Cabinet 1921; the last in my cellar, as I just had the decency to refrain from mentioning. Max noticed what he ate and drank, so I wish I could recall what my adoring forethought had ordered for him to eat with the Steinberg Cabinet. Can we have started with turtle soup? This is not merely a random suggestion; among the treasures in my knife-box, and even more lovingly hoarded than the illustrated ties, I have a letter from him about my Matriarch books, comparing their "full rich milieu" to turtle soup:

> "—*thick* turtle soup— of which one doesn't merely sip one's plateful to the end. Say, rather, a great lake of T.T.S. in which one swims warmly at one's leisure, swallowing from time to time gratefully and without indigestion one of the lumps of green fat that float so prodigally on its surface."

A tribute, I thought, to the spirituality of my work ... until in my recent mood of despondency, I was attacked by morbid misgivings: did he actually state in so many words that he was addicted to turtle soup? Supposing I were to write to a young author, comparing his book to toad-in-the-hole—"Not just a meager helping of toad-in-the-hole, but a great golden spread of batter with dozens of spicy little nuggets of sausage nestling hotly in their holes" ... still that need not mean that I liked toad-in-the-hole. Which I don't.

Because I never tired of reading Max, the Steinberg Cabinet '21 gave me courage to attack him for his laziness in not producing more; telling him he should not cease from mental strife—His defense was almost too ingenious to be convincing:

"You see, the truth is that I can *only* write with a quill pen, and where I live in Italy there are no geese."

> (Au clair de la lune,
> Pierrot répondit:
> 'Je n'ai pas de plume,
> Je suis dans mon lit.')

It was on this same occasion, after dinner, after the wine, that I recall Max standing on his head, his wife protesting but not enough to deter him; for he was bent on illustrating some story, though I cannot remember what it was, which required his two legs precariously lifted into the air and wobbling in the shape of a V. "It's a Wee, Granpa, it's a Wee!" I wanted to shout, irresistibly reminded of Louisa Alcott's *Good Wives*, where she describes her father doing the same to instruct Meg's little son Demi in the alphabet.

In spite of his sophistication in the ways of the world and the astringent outlook expressed in the devastating remarks scrawled in the corner of his cartoons, there was a delightfully childlike quality about Max. Philip Guedalla had a fine collection of original Beerbohms which he had hung along his hall and the whole way up the stairs; and a prettier sight I have rarely seen than their creator, at what must have been his first visit to the house, being coaxed in vain to move a little more rapidly upstairs into the drawing-room on the first floor; he cannot have seen them for a long time, because he lingered in front of each one, every line of his back expressing chubby surprise and gratification: Dear-me! well-I-never! was-I-really-all-that-brilliant?

That must have been one of my lucky periods, because I kept on finding myself seated beside him at these small, intimate dinner-parties; and when in recent years I laboriously try to assemble causes for gratitude to set against our innumerable frustrations and woes, this should surely be set high in the list. For again I found him beside me, this time at a dinner-party in a studio, with a door accidentally left ajar to disclose a glimpse of the charming, voluptuous bedroom of our charming, voluptuous hostess. It happened that he and I were discussing our favorite bedside literature: "*How* do you read in bed?" I inquired, interested in every detail of my hero's home life. "I mean, what position do you find most comfortable? Do you prop yourself up with a lot of pillows behind you? Or lie on your side, supported on your elbow? Or do you lie flat on your stomach with the book on the pillow?" Max thought it over, began to speak, stopped, thought again, and then with a wistful look towards the bedroom, and confidentially as though some character in Boccaccio were planning a roguish incident to interrupt his monkish career: "Do you know, I'm afraid I shall have to ask our hostess if I may go to bed before I can show you."

My instinct of self-protection must have bidden me forget, until now, my first meeting with Max, because I did make the most awful ass of myself. Once more at a dinner-party; a huge dinner-party given by the American publisher Russell Doubleday in a suite of rooms at one of our great hotels, I think they were called King Charles's Rooms, where one led to another in an endless chain, a sequence of narrow refectory tables stretching through. It must have been just as a bell rang summoning us all to take our seats, that Rebecca West, knowing better than any Carlyle how I felt on Heroes and Hero-worship, dashed up to me and said: "Come along, I want you to meet Max Beerbohm!" and I had had no time to pull

myself together before I found myself being introduced.
I had not the sense to realize there was really no necessity
to think out something especially brilliant as an opening
display of virtuosity, and that "how are you keeping"
or "pleased to meet you" would have done better than
my ultimate choice . . . For gazing down the long per-
spective of white table-cloths to where at the top of the
table in the farthest room sat Russell Doubleday—(the
only person so far to have taken his seat, probably in the
hope of inducing his guests to stop lingering)—and noticing that at this distance he looked like the vanishing-point
at which parallel lines were ultimately supposed to meet,
and wanting to insure that my witty comparison taken
from art classes at school would be thoroughly under-
stood, I said: "Have you ever learnt how to draw, Mr.
Beerbohm?"

Neither more nor less than that. "Have you ever learnt
how to draw, Mr. Beerbohm?"

Review of *Sir Max Beerbohm*—Bibliographical Notes
by A. E. Gallatin.

Bibliography should be, as in this instance, of satisfying completeness and of sober and seemly appearance.
A bibliography presupposes a solemn absorption in its
theme to the exclusion of everything else, similar to having your portrait painted, but nicer, because you need
not be present yourself. Its dignified adherence to facts
compares well with the more modern ways of its kins-
man, biography, which grows freakish in the twentieth
century. You cannot play ducks and drakes in a bibliography; you cannot be apocryphal; you cannot be in-
accurate; you cannot take sides.

Here I stopped, bewildered; maternal instinct giving evidence that this extract from a few torn pages, typed and clipped together and put away in an old folder, must have been written by myself; and although memory cannot definitely affirm having seeen the stuff in print signed G. B. Stern, I could not with any certainty repudiate it. I went on reading, and of parts of it I thought: "This is pretty awful, I hope it *isn't* by me," but once or twice: "This is *better* than me!" Presently, blushing, I laid it down rather hurriedly . . .

> Bibliography is a symbolic coronation. Reverence walks backwards in front of it, deeply bowing. It comes after the honor of a Uniform Edition, and stands for the final accolade.

I might as well have wound up this purple patch with "Rise, Sir Max!" and be done with it. In the faint hope that after all it had not been written in dead seriousness, I went on to the next sentence, which I think absolves me by its more familiar note of flippancy:

> We who know the symptoms of post-bibliography can observe a faint, silvery halo round the head of the embarrassed author. Then it begins to harden. Then it is there for good.

Browsing backwards (an exotic accomplishment) through John Rothenstein's Introduction to the Penguin edition of Beerbohm caricatures, I lit on: "The principal impulse behind Max's caricature, even the most savage, I believe to be *reverence*." Restraining the desire to scribble "How true!" in the margin, I went on to: "Max Beerbohm is a leisurely perfectionist who ever since his earliest years has avoided all uncongenial work."

A Perfection Box. Nothing could be more convenient when metaphorically one is having a thorough clear-out and tidy-up among writers; like suddenly being presented with a shoe suitcase to add to your luggage; a neat receptacle, where before you had possessed merely an ordinary suitcase and the shoes had to be crammed in haphazard with the rest of your things. But for a writer to qualify as King of the Perfection Box, all he creates must be equally good; he may not win his way in and leave a scatter of unworthy performances behind on the floor. Perfection and more perfection and yet again perfection and even now perfection; who has ever yet heard anyone say: "This time it isn't a vintage Beerbohm"? In an exhibition of art treasurers, I once stood entranced in front of a cartoon entitled with deceptive modesty: "Three Things Adjudged Perfect"; the trio represented by Max Beerbohm twirling in Adeline Genée's ballet-skirt while he played Pachman's fiddle (the cartoon, by the way, with its summing-up, *was* by Max). There are other adjectives, of course, as applicable: gentle, for instance: "He was a veray parfait gentil knight" . . . with the parfait gentleness of a rapier so deftly wielded that the victim knows nothing of how he died. A maxomaniac practically from birth, idly I piled up adjectives to fit this dandy of prose and pencil: fastidious, exquisite, unerring, witty, lethal, immaculate, courteous, economical, innocent—yes, innocent, the eternal wisdom of the sage and the incorrigible audacity of the urchin accompanied by the wide-eyed limpid gaze of a baby. In 1896, choosing to retire from literature at the ripe old age of twenty-four, he had his Works collected into one slim, elegant volume; to which his publisher, John Lane of the Bodley Head and the Yellow Book, added a spoof valedictory:

> "Although it was my privilege on one occasion to meet Mr. Beerbohm—at five o'clock tea—when advancing years, powerless to rob him of one shade of his wonderful urbanity, had nevertheless imprinted evidence of their flight in the pathetic stoop, and the low melancholy voice of one who, though resigned, yet yearns for the happier past. . . ."

Some forty-five years later, during the early years of the war, Sir Max, now resident in an English village, appeared to take a more cheerful view of his old age, referring to himself on the air as Gaffer Beerbohm. Listening-in to this novice, we were startled to discover that at the microphone, too, Max could achieve a perfection that transcended art; for broadcasting only for the second time in his life, he lifted his voice and before we had time to register astonishment, sweetly and badly sang us an old-fashioned music-hall song.

To dip into his works in search of an elusive quotation is rather like a drunkard lingering outside a pub while vowing he is "just architecturally interested"; nevertheless, I did seem to recall Max himself saying something, somewhere, about perfection? And presently I ran it to earth, in his Rede lecture on Lytton Strachey:

> Very exquisite literary artists seldom are men of genius. Genius tends to be careless in its strength. Genius is, by the nature of it, always in rather a hurry. Genius can't be bothered about perfection.

How perverse of him! If he were indeed a genius, how was I now to reconcile his own definition with mine? I turned a few pages, and unaware of the shock in store for me, read: "The vulgar term, a *debunker*, the term that the average writer or talker cursorily applies to Strachey, is not only vulgar, it is also silly." And in my Preface to this very volume I had spoken of Lytton Strachey as a debunker, without any idea that I was being not only vulgar but also silly. Debunker—search as I may, I can find no more elegant alternative to the word; nor does the dictionary provide me with one; nor Roget's Thesaurus. Dear reader, lend a sympathetic ear to my quandary: should I cut it out from the Preface, justifying such a pusillanimous retreat by the argument that if Max be my master, then Max knows best? Thoroughly bothered, I returned to John Rothenstein, and oh, the comfort of a fellow sinner!

> . . . not to enlarge our understanding of heroes by treating their frailties with the same degree of candour as their virtues, but to 'debunk' them, to divest them, that is to say, of all their greatness.

Perhaps Sir John had not read in 1943 what Max Beerbohm, treading distastefully among the *débris* of modern jargon, had said as long before as—like a pendulum I swung over to the title-page of the Rede lecture, for its date? Oh, yes, well . . . 1943. I wonder how I acquired this little reprint by the Cambridge University Press? (Come to that, I wonder who was Rede? No end to this research business, one confession of ignorance leading to another.)

Courage and honesty won, and I decided to leave my own Preface exactly as it was, deleting nothing. The same Max Beerbohm who had used such exquisite courtesy and understanding to say: "If two people can't agree about a third person, the one who likes him is right, always," the same Max who in reply to my fatuous remark at our first meeting, genially owned up that he had never learnt to draw and probably would have drawn a great deal better if he had, would understand my dilemma now, and send me away reassured and happy.

JOHN BETJEMAN

WHAT is it about John Betjeman that nearly all our swains commend him, and that somewhere, deep in the catacombs, the rumor goes round of a society already forming to carry banners: *"Betjeman for Laureate!"* when in the natural order of things the Royal appointment becomes vacant? What is his indefinable something? Of course, there should be no such thing as an "indefinable something"; a slipshod phrase to get ourselves out of all the hard work of tracking down what we really do mean. He himself gives us a clue: "Poems are personal and that means that they must be sincere"—(does it?). Certainly they are a projection of an intensely personal approach imaginatively relaid via a church mouse, a woman dying, a subaltern's love-song:

> Miss J. Hunter Dunn, Miss J. Hunter Dunn,
> Furnish'd and burnish'd by Aldershot sun,
> What strenuous singles we played after tea,
> We in the tournament—you against me!

Even his frequent attacks of nostalgia are not "such as moan about the retrospect," but have a sturdier quality, informed by the Betjeman idiom which will surely go down to posterity if only because as a habit once acquired, we cannot do without it—"Just hand me your Betjeman view of the Gasworks, will you? That one over there in the north-west suburb of—Ah, thanks!"

Look here, you may argue, it's just a knack! Yes, of course it is, a mere trick of scribbling colloquial verse for his own entertainment . . . if we choose to ignore the hours of meticulous work which must have gone into these fair and simple transcriptions. *Apparently* simple. Say what you like, a poet is a poet. Nor is Betjeman in the least degree afraid of having it said of him that he is no "real poet" but a celebrant of temporary things; not exactly fugitive—gas-works are unlikely to run away at Atalanta speed; and "temporary" is not quite the right word either. Where's our Roget's Thesaurus? Thorough as always, it suggests:

Transitory, transient, transitive, passing, impermanent, evanescent, flitting, vanishing, shifting, flying, provisional, provisory, temporal, cursory, galloping, short-lived, ephemeral, deciduous—

After *deciduous* I skipped half a column, and came to "before the ink is dry: here today and gone tomorrow; *non semper erit aestas; eheu, fugaces labuntur anni!* as for man, his days are as grass."

These are sobering reflections. I chose *transitory* out of the abundance of helpfulness, and returned to the study of Betjeman's undeniable influence on the younger generation . . . A friend of mine remarked that if her son (age-group thirty) were to come in and be told John Betje-

man had been lunching in this very room yesterday—
"there would be a two minutes' silence."

And indeed, yesterday John was lunching here in my
London home for the first time, though he has frequently
been to my Brambleford cottage not far from his own
house in Berkshire. I always regret that his first visits
cannot be repeated *ad infinitum*; because they afford me
a peculiar gratification, like the secret game we play with
people who are liable to say a certain thing—and then they
do say it; expectancy fulfilled. For immediately on enter-
ing, his attention is caught by whatever pictures hang on
the walls, and: "Now, who's that by? No, no, don't tell
me, let me guess!" He plants himself in front of the picture. "*Don't* tell me!" he repeats in an agony. All right,
John, I wasn't going to—(all this like a re-cap. from one
of those panel programs I've seen him do on television:
"May I say?" in the well-known little diffident voice,
over an obscure picture of some totally unrecognizable
ruins; and then gets it dead right nearly every time!). So
I stood comfortably watching him: "It must be Suffolk,
surely? No, they don't have that shade of pink on their
walls in Suffolk; more like—Don't tell me!" Eventually I
did have to tell him: "Courtyard in Chester," by Victor
Askew. And thence to an uncharacteristic Nevinson that
also had him puzzled: "The Home of the Otter." And a
cornfield by David Rolt, burning against the sky. Then
with a touch of anticipated triumph, I said: "Bet you can't
guess who painted *that*?"—Noel Coward's unsensational
view of a row of poplars against the sky, as he used to
see them from his bedroom window in Kent. John admitted that he would never have guessed and that it was
remarkably good, especially the sky behind the poplars;
"but all the same," on closer examination, "I ought to

have known it wasn't by a professional; look, these trees aren't *rooted;* they're painted to stand *on* the ground; while for instance in this one"—(*Paris Sous la Pluie*)— "d'you see? there are obviously holes cut into the pavement and the trees were planted in earth; they don't just stand on top."

When at Brambleford I led him upstairs to continue his Xavier Le Maistre prowlings—"Voyage autour de ma chambre"—I had no doubt but that he would show special enthusiasm for several English seaside pictures; for Betjeman is an English-seaside man, and some of his finest verses celebrate the rocks and beaches in North Cornwall, where over and over again, child and man, he has gone back for his holidays. Brambleford being far inland, seaside pictures are the best I can do for my own frequent sea hanker: "Miles of Sand, Dymchurch," and "The Kiosk," a very attractive picture painted somewhere on the East Coast; both in essence truly Betjeman, intimate and nostalgic; children racing down a strip of sand darkened by a passing cloud, to bathe in England's icy summer waves—("I'm *ever* so warm, Nanny; warm as warm" . . . and our teeth chattering); children building sand-castles, with mothers and fathers squatting comfortably in the shelter of a breakwater. And I relished anew that poem of his, *North Coast Recollections*, where an inarticulate schoolboy broods tenderly over his first love—

> So deep, he feels a tightening in his throat,
> So tender, he could brush away the sand
> Dried up in patches on her freckled legs,
> Could hold her gently till the stars went down,
> And if she cut herself would staunch the wound,
> Yes, even with his First Eleven scarf,

Perhaps it may be rather a shame to suggest that he encourages in himself this mood of sentiment; all the same, when I produced a small glass paper-weight with a Victorian view of Lowestoft inset, he almost swooned with rapture: period, place, esplanade, everything about it build up to what he has called his absurd topographical predilection; and "I've never been to Lowestoft!" with a visible longing to bolt off to Liverpool Street station before we had lunch. I just restrained myself from giving him the paper-weight, but it happened to possess for me happy, low-down associations not unconnected with Neptune and an overflowing cornucopia. . . .

When I took him along to "Little Triton," the house in Brambleford where my friend Marguerite Steen lives (and named after an old ship's figurehead over the porch) he first paused outside my own cottage, gave it the architectural once-over ("Don't tell me—let me guess!") and settled its period, producing meticulous reasons for pronouncing it earlier than William IV—"several years earlier; late Georgian, some of it anyhow"—and then cavorted with delight when I told him that according to legend it had once been an Inn called the Pig and Whistle, corroborated by the 15th-century church not a stone's throw away, over the stream and along the narrow lane. For the Pig and Whistle is a corruption of Pyx and Housel, as the Goat and Compasses of God Encompasseth Us, inns where in the old days pilgrims used to put up for the night.

At Little Triton there was no need for guessing, only for enthusiasm at the wonderful collection of William Nicholson's paintings on the walls. Betjeman has an immense capacity for discipleship; I have always found that all the best men at their own stuff are good at venerat-

ing creative achievement in others. When, as already related, he came to see me later on in London, and I went
through my old knife-box to display the odd scraps of
treasure and fun hoarded there, he expressed such delight
over a quick pencil sketch by William Nicholson (repre-
senting a spirited battle between St. George and the
Dragon in a Berkshire field), plus a page of rough
sketches, by John Hassall, of a merry pig insufficiently
clad in a fig-leaf, dancing and playing a whistle, which
a friend had commissioned to be made into a paper-weight
for my desk, that out of consideration for his bashfulness
I held back several "original Betjemans" from the same
repository. My father used to remark "*dankbares Publikum!*," meaning a grateful audience, about those people
who were contented to fill that rôle and surrender themselves with shouts of genuine appreciation at whatever
might be happening in the way of an informal circus.
Appreciation may rank with availability as one of the less
showy virtues; but none the less a virtue, not to wait with
unreceptive mien and impatience ill-concealed till the
other person has finished their turn of entertainment and
let you in with yours. Certainly father would have made
the comment "dankbares Publikum" had he ever seen
Betjeman's uninhibited gusto in the passive rôle of listener,
giving himself up to it physically as well, no quiet smile
twitching the corner of his lips, but rolling about in his
chair with roars of laughter, legs kicked up into the air.
Worth while being an amusing bloke when Betjeman is
around, and still more fun to join with him in sheer joie
de vivre putting on a double turn; thus was I led long
ago into spouting "Young Lochinvar" with Noel Coward,
and recently "The Burial of Sir John Moore at Corunna"
with Betjeman; well-worn, durable recitations that contain plenty of opportunity for concerted actions. I should,

however, refuse to play second fiddle in "The Bells" turn
and turn about with Betjeman, an enthusiastic campano-
logist . . . Once he came to see me at Brambleford on the
evening for bell-ringers' practice, and sat with rapt expression, every now and then congratulating me warmly
on my good luck in having this nearby tintinnabulation
and clang to rock my sitting-room; or else let fall items of
inside information that reminded me of all the pages I
skipped in an otherwise favorite thriller, *The Nine Tail-
ors.* Really, this John Betjeman is omniscient in too many
places! Diffident or not diffident, it won't wash for him
to present himself as a sort of Brother Juniper, has he
never heard that men of erudition are thin, stooping, bony,
peevish, spectacled and absent-minded? Rarely have I encountered anyone as *present-minded* as himself; the blurb
on the jacket flap of *A Few Late Chrysanthemums* rightly
remarks on the deceptive simplicity that covers extreme
technical skill, identifying himself in subject or mood with
a sports girl of the gas-lamp era, with perpendicular architecture, an old tennis racquet, a bicycle seat, a pair of
shorts, a defective chapel stove, a Morris Eight or an en-
caustic tile.

Mine eyes dazzle—and fall on the fly-leaf opposite,
where this same man of erudition and scholarship has
chosen to inscribe my volume as follows:

Peter Stern
from
her Berkshire choms

Celtic Nation- alists {
 Sean o'betjemean
 Jan Trebetjeman
 Evan ap Betjeman
 Ewan Quetjeman (Manx)
 Iain Macbetjeman
}

He seems particularly attached to Jan Trebetjeman among
this group (and indeed I prefer him myself to that dour
Highland creature Iain Macbetjeman), for I once received
a brief note merely to give me his new address; and forgetting the touch of eccentricity in the signature, threw
it over to a secretary who was working with me tem-
porarily, to enter in my address-book; and for months
afterwards when I wanted his address I hunted for it in
vain, and had to go to endless trouble to procure it in
some less direct way; until at last one day I happened upon
it conscientiously set down among the T's.

Betjeman likes being read to; among his favorite English poets are Chaucer, Swift, Cowper, Burns, Crabbe,
Hood, Tennyson, Clough and a score or so more. He also
likes reading aloud his own poems; or at least wastes no
time making tiresome objections, but stands up in front
of whomsoever it may be, and with the same paradoxical
quality of sturdy diffidence already noticed in him, like a
child who does something well in front of grownups but
doesn't allow himself to forget that he *is* still a child, will
read, for instance, *Devonshire Street, W*.1 . . . and leave
us heartbroken.

I first heard him read it from galley-proofs, in my sitting-room at Brambleford, while I watched John van
Druten exercise his capacity for hero-worship, in a state
of humility and bliss, inter-dependent because the one
need not lead the other unless your hero be kind. Many
years had passed since that moment in a villa in the South
of France—"*Aldous Huxley is in the garden!*" Since then,
a distinguished and successful dramatist in two continents,
greying a little at the temples, Johnny has not lacked for
fans of his own. Staying with me at the cottage in 1951,
he introduced me in an hour (or several hours) of en-

thusiasm to a new idol: quoting from his fantastic memory
one poem after another out of a volume called *Selected
Poems*; which undoubtedly I should have known, but
somehow with idols of my own I had hitherto missed
them, though naturally I was familiar with the name of
John Betjeman. And after Johnny had returned to
America, I had my first personal encounter with the poet
himself, and was able to announce in my next letter that
when he came over I might be able to manage an Aldous-
Huxley-is-in-the-garden for him: *"John Betjeman is in
the porch!"* By the time the meeting could be arranged,
I knew this John (as opposed to Johnny) fairly well, and
when I told him that the famous author of *Young Woodley* and a host of other plays had originally made me familiar with his poems by reciting them, yard after yard,
he was incredulous and hardly able to believe I wasn't
pulling his leg. He promised to be with us just before six;
from four o'clock onwards Johnny was restlessly roaming
from chair to chair and book to book, unable to settle
down to anything, his eyes bright with anticipation; full
of conjecture and equally full of forebodings in the nature
of he-may-not-like-me!—"Will he mind, I wonder, if I
talk to him about his work?" "No, Johnny," heartily, "I'm
sure he won't; he's awfully good about that!" (and *sotto
voce*: "Most of us are!"). Naturally Betjeman was late,
very late. His erring sense of proportion over time has
led me, the most meticulously punctual person in the
world, to judge how much I really love him by the lati-
tude I am willing to allow between the time he says he
will come and the time he actually does arrive, comfortably free from guilt; for appointments hang as loosely
on his conscience, touching nowhere, as a sagging old
jacket. At our very first meeting my affection was put

to the test almost before it began; for I had been invited to
take part in a Brains Trust at Wantage in aid of—I forget
what; Betjeman was to be in the Chair, and the members
of the team, five of us, were assembled half-an-hour before
our Chairman arrived, characteristically friendly and
shameless, proud of his new bright green coat; and though
he apologized and gave a reason for his lateness, I couldn't
feel that the apology was wrung from his heart. Nevertheless, almost at once he had us in a semi-circle, laughing
and good-tempered over the questions . . . I suppose this
is one of the aspects of charm, to dispel resentment without even knowing one has raised it. I sometimes wonder,
on the mote and beam principle, whether unpunctuality
may not be only a minor sin, and my own reaction to it
the worse sin of the two: "If *I* can be here in time—" and
"I never keep *him* waiting so why must he—?"And while
a congenitally unpunctual person enters laughing and
singing, occupied only with the moment itself and all it
represents, surprised at being confronted with cross faces,
when a congenitally punctual person once-in-a-lifetime
arrives late, his flustered, almost agonized apologies have
no charm whatsoever. It seems unfair!

Johnny was engagingly shy when I introduced them,
and so was Betjeman, but at once they were chattering
away, "throwing a West Hampstead"—a phrase that needs
explanation: van Druten was born in West Hampstead
and lived there child and boy; emphatically it would not
be true to say that he suffers from wistful nostalgia for the
long-ago, because there are few things he enjoys as intensely as re-living that period down to the smallest detail,
skipping the intervening years; his memory is phenomenal,
and he can "throw a West Hampstead" on us for hours;
or carrying it still further, when not sternly engaged in

the pursuit of his legitimate profession, can spend a tranquil afternoon on a West Hampstead pilgrimage quite by himself, and tell us about it afterwards: how he found the sweetshop where he used to spend his pocket-money and the same woman was actually there, or at least her daughter; taking the same 'bus as he used to take when it was still a horse-bus which had brought him along, cheaply speaking, for a penny, to the same terminus... I can never forget his amazement at each discovery that some small landmark he had believed must have been swept away by now, had triumphantly survived. *Recherche du temps perdu*—the English word for it would only begin to be "infantilism" had he ever let it stand in the way of current achievements, responsibilities, interests and friendships. More in the nature, then, of a pastime; never whimsical nor coy; not misty like a daydream, but with the clear, bright colors and dependable shapes of a child's picture-book; "I collect," Jane Austen used to write where now we would say "I recollect"—and that was what Johnny loved to do, re-collect. So for his friends, the phrase passed into the language: "Johnny's throwing a West Hampstead," and we use it ourselves: I can throw a beautiful West Hampstead about Holland Park where I lived till I was fourteen .

Well, I might have known beforehand (and perhaps from his poems I did) that Betjeman was the type who would revel in throwing a West Hampstead about almost every London suburb:

The suburbs . . . are now considered "funny." Some people still think Victorian industrial scenery is only fit for invective. Churches are always "funny" unless they are written about by a devotional writer. Gas-light is funny, Pont Street is funny, all sorts of places and things are funny if only the funny writers are funny about them. I love suburbs and gas-lights and Pont Street and Gothic Revival churches and mineral railways, provincial towns and Garden cities. They are, many of them, part of my background.

He could range far afield in the realms of nostalgia about almost anywhere in England; but particularly in the same direction as Johnny's Scenes of Early Childhood thus Recollected in Tranquillity, to the north and north-west of London: Hampstead, Highgate, Parliament Hill Fields, Muswell Hill and on to Pinner and Perivale ... The two men were about the same age too, just short of fifty, so I might have foreseen I could have small share in their bean-feast except to listen and look benevolent, while they carried on, passionately absorbed in chatter of lemonade, sweets, 'bus-fares, marbles, picture papers of the period, exultant at how little they had spent and what a lot they had got for it ... Or is my psychology wrong, and were they so far steeped in their past that their sense of values had also shifted and it did not seem to them that they were spending very little, but right up to the limits of their weekly pocket-money?

And then they made a plan, I forget who first suggested it, to throw a West Hampstead together: take a day off and go for a long expedition, covering by 'bus and on foot all the surviving landmarks. "Tuesday or Wednesday next week?" "Right, call it Tuesday!" I wasn't envious, preferring to throw my companionable West Hampsteads from an armchair, and to leave out the acid-drops and glass of sticky, sweet lemonade. Presently Betjeman got up, and in that diffident manner already familiar to me,

implying please-say-if-you'd-rather-not, confessed that
out in the car he had the proofs of his new volume of
poems: "If you'd care to hear—?" Would Johnny *care*
to hear! So Betjeman fetched the galleys of *A Few Late
Chrysanthemums*, and as I have already told you, dear
children, that was when I first heard the great man read
aloud...

> Not my vegetarian dinner,
> Not my lime-juice minus gin,
> Quite can drown a faint conviction
> That we may be born in Sin.

... It must have been about twenty past seven when I
thought the moment had come to interrupt the Penny
Reading by inviting Betjeman to stay for supper, but he
said he was due home to receive a week-end guest arriving
from London by the 7:55 at Didcot: "How long will it
take him to drive out from the station? Need I start yet?"
"It should take him roughly as long from the station as
it will take you from here," I replied, "so you've got
another half-hour." Relieved that there was no hurry, he
read us "Business Girls," and "Middlesex" and "Sunday
Morning, Kings Cambridge"; and then as a parting gift
offered the proofs to Johnny because he himself had
another copy at home—"If you'd care to have them?"
When I say a parting gift, that is a polite euphemism; I
had to remind him twice more of his obligations as a host
before Little Happy-go-lucky set off at 8:15...

"See you on Tuesday, then? Look here, you do mean it,
don't you? We're really going to do this? Good. What
time shall we start? Eleven? Earlier? Half-past ten?

Would it be best for me to pick you up, or the other way around?" He mentioned his address in Paddington. "Where do you hang out when you're in London?"

A long pause. Johnny's expenses were paid by his management whenever he came over from the U.S.A. to produce. He looked down, blushed, fidgetted . . . And in a still small voice whispered: "The Ritz."

* * * *

Yet for Betjeman at any age, life was not all lemonade and 'bus-rides. A sediment of horror from his early life, never quite dispersed, rises to the surface in some of his poems; he must have endured truly appalling moments to account for the shuddering realization that though by now he may have escaped himself, for others the sickness of terror and pain are still going on. When a type of cruel, bullying schoolboy grows up still unaware of what agony he has inflicted, he ought to be forcibly fed with Betjeman's "Original Sin on the Sussex Coast" and similar delicatessen; they shouldn't be allowed to get away with it scot free . . . This is what certain of his poems do to us, make us feel revengeful! Of course, we don't even know that such experiences have actually happened to him; he may have suffered them vicariously, or imagined them, as in "Beside the Seaside" he imagined the tragedy of Jennifer:

> Which ate into her soul and made her take
> To secretarial work in later life
> In a department of the Board of Trade.

Jennifer, queen of rounders-on-the-sands the summer before, and this year deposed, carelessly flung aside:

> Timidly she goes.
> Timid and proud, for the last time a child
> "Can *we* play, Mr. Pedder?" But his eyes
> Are out to where, among the tousled heads,
> He sees the golden curls of Christabel.
> "Can *we* play, Mr. Pedder?" So he turns.
> "*Who* have we here?" The jolly, jolly voice,
> The same but not the same. "*Who* have we here?
> The Rawlings children! Yes, of course you may,
> Join that side, children, under Christabel."
> No friendly wallop on the B.T.M.
> No loving arm-squeeze and no special look.
> Oh darting heartburn, under *Christabel*!

I asked John if Jennifer were a real child and he said
no, but it was the sort of thing that might easily have
happened: "I expect I was Mr. Pedder." But of course
he couldn't have been Mr. Pedder even by empathy, or
Mr. Pedder would have been John Betjeman and unable
to be experiencing Jennifer's disillusion at the moment of
its impact. Humiliations of one's childhood are so poignant that one can be profoundly thankful he was spared
until—how long afterwards did he apply to himself the
comment of his juvenile hostess's mother at an enchanted
party he recalls in another poem of this genre?

> Oh who can say how subtle and safe one feels
> Shod in one's children's sandals from Daniel Neal's,
> Clad in one's party clothes made of stuff from Heals?
> And who can still one's thrill at the candle shine

On cakes and ices and jelly and blackcurrant wine
And the warm little feel of my hostess's hand in mine?
Can I forget my delight at the conjuring show?
And wasn't I proud that I was the last to go?
Too over-excited and pleased with myself to know
That the words I heard my hostess's mother employ
To a guest departing, would ever diminish my joy,
I wonder where Julia found that strange, rather
common little boy?

That a sense of inferiority existed, we know on his own admission of belonging to those—

"who do not drink wisely to enjoy the taste of a good drink, but solely to try and soften their sense of inadequacy, and I am often in this class. At a certain state that part of the mind which directs the functions of consideration for other disappears. The man is then his real appalling self. He *must* claim your attention."

Fortunately for us, his readers, he has claimed it with poetry; the inferiority we suspect was engendered in him as a child and an adolescent, has never been allowed to become a handicap, because he has recognized and externalized it (I almost said immortalized, but given a chance he would be sure to cross out the word). An inferiority complex must be concerned with nourishing itself by every wounding remark, every casual incident, changing them into a nice large dish of fattening food for the ego; but that avenging angel who inhabits Betjeman suddenly transforms his diffidence into a crusading force, functioning in passionate pity for the meager lives this age has inflicted on some of its sadder children. How strangely he minds, or let us say rather with what horror he remembers having been sacked three times in his earlier struggles to get a foothold; a horror later to be manifested in his vision of dreary lives lived out in a bleak room in a joyless suburb, with oilcloth on the floor and geyser ventilators . . . *Business Girls* having baths in Camden Town, where every detail of our shoddy civilization is picked out as though by a painter of Dutch interiors; picked out and denounced. His bite, however, is not *worse* than his bark—about fifty-fifty. John Sparrow, in a Preface to Betjeman's *Selected Poems*, says that satire is not his forte: "He possesses all the gifts that make a satirist except the gift of imagination." And Betjeman himself admits it to be sound advice when intelligent critics advise him to keep off satire and anger. I agree with neither, and welcome his generous rages equally with his blander type of irony apparently conceived in simple and innocent mood; I wonder why he regrets castigating those pachyderms responsible for "civilization" as it emerges in local tragedies, beauty defaced, shoved aside, destroyed to make room for "improvement."

> For human beings only do
> What their religion tells them to.
> They read the Bible every day
> And always, night and morning, pray,
> And just like me, the good church mouse,
> Worship each week in God's own house.
> But all the same it's strange to me
> How very full the church can be
> With people I don't see at all
> Except at Harvest Festival.

With Betjeman's unrivalled gift for detail he combines an insatiable curiosity in contemplating his fellow-humans

to find out what makes them tick; I am inclined to believe
that he is relieved when not seeing or hearing anything
that must arouse his compassion, so that he can let his
natural high spirits bubble over into nonsense and mischievous parody; especially where inspired by some peculiar fascination in the pearly platitudes of a certain Victorian writer of verse, Mr. Henry Wadsworth Longfellow. Twice he has put on record his brilliant assimilation
of Longfellow's own pedestrian meter; data and cliches
delivered in a flat informative New England accent. Thus
Longfellow at Venice:

All its streets are made of water, all its homes
                                    are brick and stone,
Yet it has a picturesqueness which is justly
                                    all its own.
Here the youthful Giòrgione gazed upon the
                                    domes and towers,
And interpreted his era in a way which pleases ours.

Ibsen's Pastor Brand enjoined his creed "All or nothing!" on every character who couldn't get away fast
enough; so of Betjeman's other gorgeous Longfellow
burlesque, showing that eminent poet on a visit to Mr. and
Mrs. Henry Wood in their home at Gomshall, it will have
to be, I am afraid, nothing, not even an excerpt from the
footnotes improvised by Mr. Betjeman so plausibly that
I am not sure if I can resist asking him in confidence how
much of it is *really* a "Literary Discovery"? Those footnotes!—what are the puzzled scholars of A.D. 2057 likely
to make of their exact meaning without school editions
of Betjeman with fifty pages of explanatory notes to every
fifteen of the poems themselves? Abundant notes will be

required, too, for conscientious study of another set of verses which have recently achieved wide popularity: "How to Get on in Society," beginning: " 'Phone for the fish-knives, Norman" . . . A bit bothered by my own ill-bred reluctance to give up knives and use only forks to eat my fish, I reminded John of the ancient Chinese proverb: *Soggy bread cuts no salmon;* and he replied in defiant agreement that as he was himself a bourgeois he would continue to behave bourgeois at table, knife and fork and spoon and pusher with his fish, when and how he pleased.

Cicerone of the contemporary scene and spirit, he defends his attitude in a preface to the collection *Old Lights for New Chancels*:

> Until the middle of the nineteenth century poets who wrote in the visual manner confined themselves for the most part to descriptions of nature. This was because natural scenery was more in evidence than it is now. The tradition has died hard and it is still thought by some people that all visual poetry should mention stocks and wains and elderberry bushes. . . .

We see the fabric of his verse held down, as it were, by a quantity of bright, sharp little drawing-pins—Post Toasties; Mum the Persil user; Fuller's angel cake; Robertson's marmalade and Liberty's lampshade; the MacFisheries; "there's no one to go to Freemans to ask if the shoes are done"; a Bravington ring and—

> Well-cut Windsmoor flapping lightly,
>   Jacqmar scarf of mauve and green
> Hiding hair which, Friday nightly,
>   Delicately drowns in Drene.

It has been argued, maybe justifiably, that these jingles
are not true poetry, but their value lies elsewhere; the
compassionate heart speaks for those who cannot speak
for themselves, by lifting their slogans and advertisements.
Yet—no true poet? Then what do we call this?

> Forced by the backwash, see the nearest wave
> Rise to a wall of huge translucent green
> And crumble into spray along the top
> Blown seaward by the land-breeze. Now she breaks
> And in an arch of thunder plunges down
> To burst and tumble, foam on top of foam,
> Criss-crossing, baffled, sucked and shot again,
> A waterfall of whiteness, down a rock,
> Without a source but rollers' further reach:
> And tufts of sea-pink, high and dry for years,
> Are flooded out of ledges, boulders seem
> No bigger than a pebble washed about
> In this tremendous tide.

And this:

> And London shops on Christmas Eve
>   Are strung with silver bells and flowers
> As hurrying clerks the City leave
>   To pigeon-haunted classic towers,
> And marbled clouds go scudding by
> The many-steepled London sky.
>
> And is it true? And is it true,
>   This most tremendous tale of all,
> Seen in a stained-glass window's hue,
>   A Baby in an ox's stall?
> The Maker of the stars and sea
> Became a Child on earth for me?

"Well, *I* think it's far better to do good to your fellow-creatures than just go in for churchiness!"—how often have we heard that completely idiotic alternative offered as though it were a *sine qua non* that the one must necessarily exclude the other? Betjeman is an inspiring proof that they can dwell together in perfect harmony. Perhaps if we were to define his constant pre-occupation with ecclesiastical architecture as an absorbing hobby, and that tender understanding of his fellow-creatures as his life, we would come somewhere near the truth. For religion lies at the heart of his loveliest poems, and in his vernacular "the local" might just as well be the nearest church as the nearest Inn.

SHEILA KAYE-SMITH

THREE WAYS HOME was actually Sheila Kaye-Smith's third autobiography; her first, though few may realize it, was that enchanting book about her childhood, *The Children's Summer* which ended with "Selina's" passionate prayer: "Oh God, please one day may I always live in the country!"—characteristic of those beliefs to which she was to remain forever constant and unchanging: God, and natural things through God. In these pages, and in their sequel *Selina is Older*, we can watch a highly strung, swiftly elated, often rebellious little girl tormented by her wish somehow to please God by voluntary sacrifice, instead of merely conforming to the voices of Nurse and Mother telling her she could best please Him by being good and obedient. When Nurse was summoned away at her father's death—

"Mother, I can't go to sleep. I'm too excited."
"Excited about what?"
"About God dying for Nurse's father."

"Sssh," said Mother firmly.

"But Mother, I *am* excited. Why mayn't I be?"

"People aren't meant to be excited about such things."

But Sheila-disguised-as-Selina was far nearer a mystical response to life: she went on being excited:

> He died for everyone, she knew, so every time a person died He came to earth and did it again. He was now on earth, living and dying for Nurse's father. Then He would go back to Heaven till someone else died.

And in that last sentence we get a glint of humor slanted from a mature Sheila Kaye-Smith on to her eight-year-old conception of how it all worked.

If I seem to lay undue stress on *The Children's Summer* and *Selina is Older*, it is because re-reading them now, I am amazed how they provide a vivid blueprint for her whole career in theological adventure; the embryonic writer, too, is seen making significant discoveries— ("Mother, can you eggsplain something? Why is it that when I write a play it's different to what was in my mind, and when I act it it's still more different?"). As an instance of reality impinging on pure imagination, Selina had found extraordinary satisfaction in composing a Beautiful Poem on the tragic theme of Nurse's absence; until Nurse came back "looking strange and different," and standing just inside the nursery door, suddenly burst into tears. A grown-up person *crying*? For the first time Selina realized grief and loss and death; and all the comfort of literary creation failed her; she did not want to go on with her Beautiful Poem; it seemed inadequate.

Nevertheless, God continued to mix Himself up in the

oddest way with her small busy affairs of every day. She was not above a utilitarian application of her faith, and having prayed in an ectasy of desire for a certain glamorous doll's-toilet-set hanging on a Christmas tree at a party, she walked straight up to the little girl to whom it was eventually handed, and said: "Don't you think God would want you to give me that toilet-set?" That time it came off. But on an occasion when she refused to sing comic songs on a Sunday though her younger sister "Moira" threw scruples away and thereby won a crackly pear as a prize—"Oh Lord," Selina prayed fervently, "send *me* a pear—a *crackly* pear!" She likewise prayed in vain for a toy tortoise to emerge from her Surprise Packet bought at the village shop, and again had to learn how God did not respond to prayer with an instant rain of unripe fruit and tortoises.

Grown-ups of that late Victorian era did their best, within limits, to make their children happy; but beyond a few pious formulae in the style of the Elsie Books, they rarely perceived what was spiritually required of them. One character, however, does appear in these pages, a lady visitor who actually listened with respectful attention while Selina babbled on for hours about her dream playmate who "dressed in gold and silver flowers, and lived alone and did exactly as she liked." Sometimes she wondered whether perhaps she ought to tell Miss Elder that the heroine of her fantasy was "only a made-up little girl," but she could not bring herself to do it . . . Until one Sunday the curate preached about those hardened sinners who tell lies for the love of lying—"so that in the end they did not know which was the lie and which was the truth." A pity that Mr. Oxford could not grasp how mysteriously the mind of an author worked on its material, the oak nascent in the acorn. Amid tears and anguish, shame and terror, Selina confessed her "sin" to Miss Elder and got ready absolution: "Miss Elder, she isn't in a story, but she's a little girl I tell stories about. Do you see?"

Sheila's father was a busy doctor with his practice in St. Leonards, a seaside resort on the South Coast near Hastings, which she later immortalized in a haunting novel, *Tamarisk Town*; to my mind, the prize-winner in her first ten years of writing. Their house stood in a road with houses on either side; but for a few blissful months every summer the two children and their Nurse were sent to stay on a farm inland; and all through the rest of the year she yearned towards this haven of freedom among fields and flowers. Saying goodbye to it each time was a tearing agony; and autumn and winter and spring were dim, grey seasons of banishment and nostalgia, only brightened by "the gleam of Platnix Farm" coming gradually nearer again, promising a renewal of her paradise. Once she spent a precious penny on a rather withered bunch of primroses offered for sale in the street, simply because their fading sweetness evoked haunting memories of her beloved Platnix; but then for reasons characteristically Sheila, immediately presented them to an organgrinder who, disgusted, threw them into the road to be crushed by an oncoming van. Again a storm of brokenhearted weeping . . . while Mother suggested to her foolish, over-impetuous little daughter that next time she wanted to be kind to a poor person—"I *don't* want to be kind to a poor person. I want to give something to God. I want to give Him something of my own." And when Mother tried to elaborate on the usual tiresome theme that religion meant not being naughty and not answering back and not hitting her little sister and so forth, she could have no idea how behind Sheila's quiescence was outrage at thus placing "the powerful and exciting Creator of the world" among all these nursery platitudes.

Her urgent need to "give Him something of my own," evidence of her compulsion to offer up visible tokens in worship and thankfulness, proved of the same durable quality as that less agreeable troop of funny infantile phobias and fears and shrinkings which were first chronicled in *The Children's Summer* and accompanied her for the rest of her life: she used to get hysterical if the water started to gurgle down the plug-hole in her bath before she had time to rush from the bathroom; she would not walk in the shade of dark trees if she could help it, nor go anywhere near buildings that had been burned down—the sour scorched smell was in itself a horror.

Her childish "treats" she looked forward to with trembling excitement, and as she grew older, had to learn that the rapture of anticipation would usually end in disillusion. Perhaps her later reactions to so many childish disappointments, her dread of leaving home even to go on holiday in France—"though I *love* it when I'm there"—her social evasions and refusals, work back to the unspoken longing for something *whole* that would be with her for ever, completely satisfying.

And always she was a natural story-teller, a spinner of yarns. When she was three years old she used to walk round and round her parents' bedroom while they drank their early tea, pretending to read out of a book; and her husband recalls that when they first got married and he could spare time from arduous work in his London parish, they used to go for long walks in the country, and at any moment she would start telling him a story; and

again how his brother John came to supper with them
on Sunday nights, and always asked her for a story before
he went home; and she never thought them up beforehand: on one occasion without a cue she began: "Dulci-
bella Gurling was bicycling along the road to the village,
and suddenly . . ." thus the evening's story was launched.

Professionally her reputation was achieved as a regional
novelist; which meant that at her every attempt to set
a tale outside Sussex, in any other part of England or the
world, there was an outcry from her readers; yet her
bold imagination won a gratifying tribute from a stranger
who recognized her in a Hastings bus and at once burst
into warm praise of her new book, *A Challenge to Sirius*,
and particularly of the section placed in Yucatan: "You
see, I've lived in Yucatan most of my life, so I can judge
how well you must know it!" Her first book, *The Tramp-
ing Methodist*, found a publisher when she was only
twenty; that and her next two were not laid in present-
day Sussex, but in the raffish period of the smuggler and
highwayman, the vagabonds of the roads. There is nearly
always a tendency in critics—(and not only in critics)—
to look back regretfully on a writer's youthful work,
mistaking promise for the high noon of achievement; and
in the case of such a very young writer as Sheila, they
were especially struck by her unusual gusto and masculine
boldness. Most of our first novels at that time were inclined to be whimsical and "pierrotic," but Sheila went
to the other extreme: picaresque, yes; picturesque, definitely no. At the start of her career, that excellent novelist
W. L. George, then her greatest friend, encouraged her
when encouragement was most needed, and gave her the
ideas for two robust successes, *Sussex Gorse* and later
Joanna Godden; he wrote with high approval of "the

virility, the cognizance of oath and beer, of rotating crop, sweating horse, account book, vote and snickersnee that Sheila Kaye-Smith exhibits in her novels," and then went on to describe her appearance as though she had been fashioned wilfully to contradict the manner and forceful-ness of her writing . . . "very thin, with a grace all made of quiescence, her eyes gray and retracted a little, as if always in pain because man is not so beautiful as the earth that bore him." Full recognition came with *Sussex Gorse*, which struck deep into the soil instead of restlessly tramp-ing and galloping over its surface; its protagonist, Reuben Backfield, gave his entire life to possess and dominate Boarzell Common, a tough stretch of moorland on which it was supposed that naught save gorse could grow. I wonder how often Sheila was asked "Why don't you give us another Sussex Gorse?" (we agreed on our difficulty in restraining an eldritch scream at compliments begin-ning "Why don't you give us another . . ."). Her first best-seller, *Joanna Godden*, appeared in 1921. It took all Willie George's influence to bring Sheila to abandon her powerful, ruthless, lusty men, and concern herself instead with the fortunes of a woman. And henceforth it was "Why don't you give us another Joanna Godden?" till in turn replaced by ". . . another End of the House of Alard?" Yet her post-war novels were certainly no less accomplished. Indeed, I should say that *Mrs. Gailey* and *The View from the Parsonage* showed a clear gain in humor, shrewdness and mental breadth.

"How do you write your books?"—another question familiar to authors, more understandable than why-don't-you-give-us-another, because more likely to provide va-riety in the answer. Sheila could not dictate; she wrote every word herself with hardly any corrections. Her hus-

band—(I must be allowed to speak of him as Penrose, because he too is a close friend of mine)—Penrose often
tried to persuade her to dictate to a secretary, so that she
need not get so tired. "Oh *no*, I couldn't, she'd look at
me!" She had to have long, silent periods of gestation; an
idea for a book would sink deep down into her subconscious and remain there for many years before she
ever used it. Once Penrose told her of an amusing incident,
and when a decade later it came into a novel, she did not
even remember that it had originated with him. And
when she was commissioned to contribute a volume on
the Kent and Sussex Weald for a Regional Series, all she
had to do, according to Penrose, was revive what material lay submerged from when she was a young girl and
used to bicycle by herself all over the Kent and Sussex
borders. Helpfully he motored her round to explore out
lying villages, and she would verify her memories ("I
want to make sure that old XVth century house is next
to the church, and not at the other end of the village
green . . . it's some time since I was there. . . .") and then
he supposed there was nothing more to see on that expedition, but she pleaded that she just wanted to sit down
alone for a bit and "let it soak in." But it was not really
a question of soaking in; she had to have solitude while
her bones reminded her of what she already knew.

For she revelled in solitude. Her need for it was positive
and strong. While at home in St. Leonards, of course she
had shared a room with her younger sister; even in a large
house it would never have occurred to Mrs. Kaye-Smith
that Sheila was a hermit. Then she married Penrose, and
they lived in Holland Park, and he would come home
from his parish work and find her sitting in her study, not
having been out all day: "It's so nice just being alone."

We who knew Sheila well and were so fond of her, had a portmanteau word, "shruddling," for her recurrent physical reaction of shrinking and huddling away from any new enterprise. Penrose had quite a job to break down her reluctance to go out, although she enjoyed parties (moderately) once she was there; enjoyed going to them more than giving them. I have seen her shruddle back from the most unalarming form of human contact, yet her refusal to quit their Sussex home, dangerously situated in "Bomb Alley" during the Blitz of 1940, while Penrose was constantly called out on fire-fighting duty for hours and hours of the day and night, was in heroic contradiction to little Selina's panics; for she had never outgrown her terror of explosive noises; and as in childhood her fingers were at once stuffed into her ears when the moment was at hand for pulling crackers at a party, in her adult years you could still never get her to the theater if she were warned beforehand that somebody might fire a gun in the course of the play. Nevertheless, with the German planes constantly passing overhead going to London, and unloading their bombs on the way back, she occupied the apprehensive hours by teaching herself to cook. And the unnatural fastidiousness which had made her such a choosey, difficult child at meals, was just what was required half a century later to turn her into a first-class chef; she did not excel in "good plain cooking"; it was the theory of cooking that interested her, and experimenting with recipes mostly from French cookery books. The de la Condamines, her mother's family, were Huguenot refugees who had settled in Guernsey and probably bequeathed her a love of France and everything French.

Life changed for both Sheila and Penrose when in 1929

they discovered to their joy that each had been keeping from the other a conviction that they had to become Roman Catholics. That meant lay service for him; as a married man he could no longer remain a priest. But for Sheila, apart from its spiritual implications, the transition spelt an end to at least one panic, that at any moment his ministry might necessitate a move to a town uglier than London and even further away from her beloved Sussex. Her job on the contrary had no strings to it; she could write anywhere, given quietness and a room of her own. So they converted an old oast-house among the open fields not far from the village of Northiam, and the round room downstairs became Sheila's study, looking out on the garden of Little Doucegrove. In this house she was happy for thirty-two years. She liked Penrose to bring her tea very early in the morning; breakfast was not until nine, but Sheila wanted tea at seven-thirty so that she could lie and think and think how truly happy she was, living in the country; and plan how she would write that day's piece of her current book. She enjoyed the garden and arranging flowers and discussing what was to grow where, but unlike several women authors (for instance Lady Russell who wrote *Elizabeth and her German Garden*) she was not the type to let it possess her thoughts or her leisure, and could easily bear to delegate the actual pruning and weeding, tying-up and planting out; her love of the soil had about it an earthy quality not inconsistent with the strong mystical streak we have already noticed; and her attachment to Little Doucegrove was not a Nanny's practical form of cossetting, but a deep maternal tenderness . . . During the 1914-1918 war, she wrote a novel called *Little England*, one of her few failures from the point of view of sales and reviews; no epic,

but infused with that same maternal brooding tenderness
... Little England ... Little Doucegrove:

> Little Doucegrove, a farm which plays an important
> part in my early novel *Spell Land*, is one of the many
> in this corner of Sussex which owes its origin to French
> settlers entering the country as Huguenot refugees.
> Robert Douce, a native of Beauface, was woodcutter
> and miner to Sir William Sidney at the furnace of Pan-
> ningridge, near Salehurst, and was granted letters of
> denization in 1554, in the name of Douce or Dows.
> Doucegrove, in the heart of the Sussex iron country,
> may well have been a settlement for his descendants.
> The first half of the name is pronounced Dows, and
> the second is probably an eighteenth century embellish-
> ment (the place on one ancient map appeared as Holm-
> grove, and until quite recently was sometimes known
> as Petty Doo), for it certainly does not date back far
> enough to be a corruption of the Saxon gryfja, for pit
> (as in Skinningrove), though there is a field close to the
> house still known as the Pit Field.

Here she settled down; "settled" as defined by the dictionary: *placed in a permanent condition*. Although an
incongruous streak in her nature cared about clothes and
talk of clothes and could spend a lot of money choosing
them without reproaching herself for extravagance, she
could very well do without pavement shopping and
parties and the theater; they were interruptions, not es-
sentials. And it must be admitted that she could do without friends; she did not need her fellow-creatures, apart
from Penrose. The truth was that she loved very few
people, and when she did, required no constant contact

with them; when they had her love, they had it for good no matter what they did or how seldom they met. Her instinct preferred those with tremendous vitality, capable of breaking down her defenses without appearing to notice them; preferred, in fact, gate-crashers. She herself could never make advances . . . except to cats; her particular affection for cats probably sprang from appreciation of their independence and *style*; she was amused, not wistful, that they sought her lap only to make themselves comfortable; and when their mood rejected her loving overtures, she took it as a sign of affinity, not of failure.

Our first encounter happened during the World War of 1914 1918. I had to overcome my respect for a contemporary who was already author of four published books to my one; but there was nothing formidable to distinguish this thin, frail girl in a scarlet pullover, from a hundred other similar young women with long, thin legs in black stockings and brown hair softly bobbed . . . until, like W. L. George, I began to notice the strange way that every now and then her eyes seemed to recede as though she were withdrawing herself from human company and no longer aware it existed. I was her intimate friend for some forty years, but every time we met I felt like a housebreaker who could not immediately find the combination of the safe. Fundamentally her character and tastes were more virile than mine, and her favorite authors tough and uncompromising, as emerged from her collection of reminiscences published posthumously, *All the Books of My Life*. And though her passionate delight in Jane Austen might seem to contradict this preference, it was born, I think, by virtue of Miss Austen's unsentimental judgments, her clear appraisal of falsity and weakness; for Sheila herself was impatient of softness and sentimentality, and her realistic outlook occasionally expressed itself with startling vigor.

I may have been about twenty-five or twenty-six when she and I went down together to stay for a week at Bradenham, a charming village not far from where Lord Beaconsfield had lived and died. Thrift Cottage stood on the edge of the green with a view across to the church. The gorse was out on Naphill Common not far away, and so was the washing, brilliant white spread on the bright yellow. But surely we would never have brought only one book each, to carry us over seven days and evenings in rainy England? My highbrow choice was *The Brook Kerith* by George Moore. Nowadays, caring less for opinion, I might easily have accompanied *The Brook Kerith* with a little light relief—an Agatha Christie, say, or a P. G. Wodehouse. What made it more hazardous was that I had never read George Moore before, and *The Brook Kerith* his initial experiment in leaving out all punctuation and inverted commas; you can imagine how I felt, struggling along through the first chapters. Then Sheila came to the rescue, and but for her (and but for George Moore) I might never have become the lover of Jane I am now. Sheila, I found to my astonishment, whatever additional books companioned her on far travels to Bradenham or elsewhere, never moved without a volume of Jane Austen; this time it happened to be *Emma*, and she offered to lend it to me while she read her library equivalent of *The Brook Kerith*. Better than nothing, I thought, little knowing. And began:

> Emma Woodhouse, handsome, clever and rich, with a comfortable home and happy disposition, seemed to unite some of the best blessings of existence, and had

lived nearly twenty-one years in the world with very little to distress or vex her.

Wholly and without reservation, I surrendered to the spell of Jane Austen; and henceforth whenever we were together, Sheila and I, we "talked Jane." We could not help ourselves. So that when Foyles gave a Jane Austen luncheon and we were asked to speak, I took the opportunity to pay what I hope was a graceful tribute to Sheila's husband (not a Janeite) for all he had endured without loss of temper or tolerance; for he always made me welcome at Little Doucegrove, though it meant, so to speak, that directly that woman came into the house, his wife would be at the bottle again! At last, from merciful motives, we had the notion of collaborating to write a book, not so much about Jane Austen as an informal record of these endless conversations.

People are interested in collaboration. They frequently asked us how we did it; usually adding that they were sure *they* never could! But we did not collaborate in any literal or visual sense, one of us busily writing and the other leaning over her shoulder and offering suggestions, and then after an hour or two changing places; we sat comfortably in armchairs over the fire, and as we had always done, brought forth various aspects in Jane Austen's half-dozen masterpieces: her characters, themes, scenes, tendencies; and then amiably divided them up according to our dispositions, each of us to be responsible for alternate chapters; once or twice not quite so amiably, when we both tried to bag the same chapter; then it had to be: "All right, I'll give it to you, provided *I* can have . . ." But on the whole our desires were different because luckily they were governed by very different special proficiencies: Sheila excelled by her remarkable sense of period and history; she had read more widely—and wisely —than I; to her, research had no dry connotations; for her scholarship on so many subjects and so lightly carried, was amazing; she read the most learned works from choice, not from a sense of duty, sending for modern French and English theology and psychology as they came out. She had desired an academic life and begged her father to send her to Girton, but Dr. Kaye-Smith refused; he thought it would be too much for the highly-strung little daughter so dear to him; and no doubt he was right. But research only appealed to me if it came along accidentally; and the eighteenth and nineteenth centuries had never appealed to me as to Sheila; I rejoiced in Jane Austen's characters and her dialogue and her characters giving themselves away by their dialogue—and every now and then Jane Austen giving *her*self away unawares, as every author is liable to do when off guard. And of course we both relished to the full her humor and irony informing every page.

But our collaboration had a sad corollary: there was no doubt that I got more fun out of the business than Sheila. Tragedy unforeseen, it killed her recreation. She had always read a few pages of Jane Austen in bed, every evening for years and years—(the same need of complete relaxation, the same confidence that here was the right food, impelled John van Druten and myself to put among *our* bedside books Sheila's own two, *The Children's Summer* and *Selina is Older*). Lazily talking about Jane Austen was one thing, but when she entered her study and sat down at her desk, she became a professional; Jane now had a fatal association with work; and for recreation she turned instead to P. G. Wodehouse.

Yet it was she, not I, who tentatively and to my surprise suggested a second volume on all the loose Jane material which had accumulated since our first. When the
sequel was mooted, we walked up and down the rose-
garden at Little Doucegrove and came near to quarrelling
over a suitable title; *Talking of Jane Austen* had come
easily, and Sheila could not at first see what was wrong
with *Still Talking of Jane Austen*. But I could hear a
chorus of critics, caustic and disparaging: "What, *still?*
They *can't* be! All this time, and those two women *still*
talking of Jane Austen!"—Finally we compromised on
More Talk of Jane Austen; "I can't see the difference,"
Sheila protested; but there was just that difference; "more
talk" could at least mean that there had been interim
periods before we started off again.

The fan-letters we received gave me a rather pathetic
picture of confirmed Janeites all over the world but never
two in the same house or neighborhood; each letter was
an outpouring from a grateful desert-islander; apparently
Jane-lovers pine and turn their faces to the wall if they
cannot swap Jane-enthusiasm, and these letters did not
concern themselves nearly as much with our ideas about
Jane, as theirs. I had over a hundred; or maybe double
that number scattered over the years, and Sheila as the
senior Janeite probably had more. I gathered from warily
comparing notes with my collaborator, that a preference
for her or for me emerged very clearly; sometimes my
correspondents expressed themselves quite frankly: "I'm
writing to you—(not *her*)—because though I devoured
every line of the book, I enjoyed your Chapters better."
And one can be sure that Sheila's mailbag contained fully
as many letters beginning, "I'm writing to you—(not
her)—"

Adam entered a world already well furnished and well organized. It was like arriving at a house which the servants had made ready for comfortable occupation. There is a passage in Jane Austen's *Sense and Sensibility* which describes the servants' delight when the long-expected family at last arrives at the cottage they have been preparing for them. Is it fanciful to picture a similar feeling of joyful relief throughout the world when at long last, after all the successive ages of its history, the master of the house appeared?

I quote from *Quartet in Heaven,* her most important contribution to Catholic literature. It consisted of four penetrating and unromanticized studies of St. Rose of Lima, St. Catherine of Genoa, St. Thérèse of Lisieux, and Mother Cornelia Connelly of Philadelphia. The book concluded with a brilliant inquiry into the Nature of Sanctity. To understand her approach to religion it must be remembered that she could not bear sentimentality and emotion; hers was unequivocally an intellectual approach, all of a piece, and Catholicism suited her so well because of its wholeness. She cared terribly about fellow Catholics who wrote to her, known or unknown; nuns of various Sisterhoods in England and the States, and converts like herself, and those hovering on the brink as yet undecided whether to come in or stay out; and she did not write to them just once out of a sense of duty and let it go at that; Penrose discovered after her death that at whatever sacrifice of time and labor, she had kept up a regular correspondence of which she never spoke to anyone. Her own conversion, described in *Three Ways Home,* was a quiet crossing over from the Anglican side of the road, when the moment came, without undue drama or agonies of indecision:

In religion I have to learn to look not outwards but inwards, and in my writing I have to learn to look not inwards but outward.

She admits that "we cannot altogether withhold our sympathy from the popular craving for the miraculous," and compares the two mystics of her quartet, St. Catherine and St. Rose, with the two non-mystical subjects, Mother Cornelia and St. Thérèse. Because these particular Saints had also vivified her mind to a delighted perception of what Hollywood would call the "story angle" of their lives on earth, she treated them as the quick, not the dead; never alienating us with any priggish nor admonitory reminder of their sainthood. To St. Thérèse de Lisieux especially, she and Penrose felt they owed a peculiar attachment for having inspired them both at the same time to join the Church of Rome; and in gratitude for the profound relief implicit in "both at the same time," they started a Mass Center, at first in a room above their garage; and in time, when the floor gave way under the large rural congregation hitherto unsuspected which seeemed to have sprung out of the very furrows for miles around, they built a church on their land, dedicated to St. Thérèse. Penrose can speak for both of them in his own autobiography, *The Making of a Layman*:

> To this end was I born, and grown and married . . . to plant an Altar in this field. It was for this that we were uprooted from all that we were doing, and set down here in Sussex. For this day God has wrought for years.

When I told Sheila many years later that I too was about to be received into the Catholic Church, her spon-

taneous joy in expressing how much she cared, moved
me more than I can say, and still does whenever I recall
it. It may have been my fancy that our old friendship had
latterly, for no particular reason except perhaps this very
need of a freshening wind, shown signs of drifting into
the doldrums. Now it was renewed; I went down far
oftener to stay at Little Doucegrove, and at my first
Christmas Midnight Mass, knelt with Sheila and Penrose
in their little church surrounded by dim, root-smelling
Sussex fields, and German prisoners (locally interned)
crowded the aisles and sang *Adeste Fideles* and *Stille
Nacht* as though they were at home, as indeed they were
that night, and so we all were, all over the world. But the
following Christmas they had gone back to their own
country, and dismayed, I asked Sheila: "Then who's going to sing?" "Why, *us*, Peter, you and me!" All very
well, but Sheila belonged to the timeless brigade of which
John van Druten and Pamela Frankau and I are perforce
members: we all love singing, and we all think the others
more out of tune than ourselves, and cannot understand
the reactions of the really musical who either shout with
laughter or implore us to stop. Sheila appeared not to see
what a difference the loss would make; but in such a small
isolated church with obviously no trained choir it was
no easy matter for a lay couple to organize everything
without a resident priest, and required endless steady de-
votion and practical labor to keep it going; yet thereby
Sheila's inner life expanded every year in a sub-soil of
rich fertility. She had known what she instinctively
needed for nourishment of the spirit; three ways home
were clearly marked out for her: writing, the country,
and her religion, and she followed them with a child's
directness.

THE LUNTS,
LYNN AND ALFRED

"THE LUNTS are wonderful, especially Lynn,"
"The Lunts are wonderful, especially Alfred"—
admittedly these two schools of thought exist,
dividing, on close investigation, into an exact fifty-fifty;
Alfred contributed one more adherent to the former
school, Lynn to the latter.

And as in her estimate of John Betjeman: "They're one
of the people who *cut ice*," said my same positive young
friend speaking for her generation. At which, amused by
use of the singular, we can agree that they are indeed a
team to end all teams; only amazed that they could ever
have achieved the feat of being born in such entirely
separate portions of the globe: Lynn at Woodford in
Essex, and Alfred in Milwaukee. During the dangerous
years of the war, they felt they had to come over and
act in England (to show that they belonged to us as well
as to the States), flying from Lisbon at a period when pas-
senger planes were constantly shot down into the sea, due

to the Germans' fond delusion that every air hostess was Winston Churchill in disguise. They were glad when we welcomed them with such warm pleasure, but surprised that anyone should be surprised . . . Surely some things are taken for granted!

The Lunts' superb attachment to the theater, not only to Art with a large capital A, but to each infinitesimal item that might be improved by hours spent on the rack of hard thinking, has resulted in every moment of their days and nights being dedicated to this single-minded passion. With the same objective sincerity, they care about their audiences; whether there are five hundred people in front, or only three in the stalls and a couple in the upper circle, that night and every night the play and the actors must give all they have; the audience of five or five hundred is entitled to it, and cheating your audience is a thing the Lunts will not stand for; they have a curious quality of innocence in their outright refusal to believe that any actor in any country of any period could commit such a crime. After a New York run of several months in Noel Coward's play *Design for Living*, they arrived at the final two performances, Saturday matinée and Saturday evening; and at the matinée, Lynn came off the stage into the wings, glowing with triumph, to announce that she had never before got her business right (it was a bit tricky) about propping up those two letters on the mantelpiece against the clock, but now, suddenly and at last, she had it to her entire satisfaction. Noel looked at her for a moment . . . and then remarked: "It's a bit late for that, isn't it, dear?" "Why *no*! There's still tonight, isn't there?" And Alfred would undoubtedly have agreed that there *was* still tonight . . . and his eyeballs would roll with that familiar startled look towards any unprofessional person who knew no better than to argue that it was "hardly worth while."

Like nearly all actors of genius, especially if they are producers as well, the Lunts will always entreat you by all they hold most dear *not* to come to their First Night, but to wait a week or two; an attitude confirmed by their peculiarly endearing behavior after a First Night. Ring them up the next morning, a little unwilling to intrude on so much thrill and glory but anxious to congratulate them on having pulled it off in a tumult of applause, innumerable curtains and a burst of reviews surpassing even their own record of good reviews, and Alfred's sad voice will reply on a note of deepest gratitude that you should even spare the time to speak a few words of comfort after such rotten acting. "We've never been as bad! Oh, we were so miserable, Lynn and I, we simply couldn't go to bed, we just sat talking . . ." Their attitude can most nearly be expressed by a child's copybook maxim about *duty*; doing their duty towards the play, towards the dramatist, towards the audience, according to their own standard; but a standard planted so high that it stays totally invisible to anyone except themselves.

It must be emphasized that all this contains not a shred of affectation or exhibitionism, no plea to be given special treatment and royal concessions; on the contrary, they truly believe in a democracy of royal concessions, and take it for granted that everyone is getting special treatment, for that is the only way they would wish it to be. Which may account for the fact that though never satisfied with less than the near-perfection to be achieved by sheer hard drive, they are invariably adored by their company; for whom, nevertheless, there are often bewildering moments when these two near-perfectionists disagree and argue *across* the actor concerned, so that his head has to turn from one side to the other, like watching at Wimbledon.

There is no star stuff-and-nonsense about the Lunts; may that be, perhaps, one reason *why* they are stars?

Until now I have tried to be austere and impersonal in my portrait, but at this point austerity breaks down; for musing on Alfred and Lynn as a team, I began to wonder if I had ever heard from them about their first meeting? No, I cannot recall a description of any such momentous, romantic scene except—yes, a casual reference from Lynn: "I was staying with his family then; we were just engaged"—one evening after supper, when Alfred's half-sister Karen and her husband from Milwaukee were in London for the Coronation; and our talk had naturally and happily turned to his boyhood and early days at Genesee in the Middle West, and to their house in the woods built in Swedish style; his mother's second husband was a Swede.

The Lunt men had all been merchants, mostly flour mills and timber. They had chinchilla rugs for their sleighs in winter—a nice extravagant touch which came into the eager reminiscences that early morning after supper in Coronation week. Alfred's father had had large ideas; he decorated the house, when he was bringing home his bride, with 30 to 40 lbs. of spices, bought wholesale; these were the quantities he was used to delivering and he could not imagine less. And five curtains to each window. And the furniture had to be machine-made, punched and decorated at every pore; you did not, at that period, bring your bride home to a house with only common hand-made furniture. Mrs. Lunt used to describe to her son the miraculous beauty of herself and her nine brothers and sisters, always to add, her voice rising in strong accusation: "And we *all* married *monsters!*"

. . . Alfred's early memories so enchanted me that I hardly dared breathe "Go on" for fear he might stop just as he was tenderly recalling the pretty voices of his little blonde sisters, Karen and Louise, every year singing their Swedish Christmas carols, cheek laid to cheek—but here Karen interrupted with a more earthy remainder of how on one occasion they had clung together, the same two little blonde sisters, ecstatically waiting for big brother to fall flat on his face, as, candle in hand, he went carefully down to the cellar to fetch up the wine, and they knew (but he did not) that the last step was not there any more.

Presently we came to a certain stark winter in Genesee when the refrain might have been "Yes, we have no chinchilla" . . . Their mother had been widowed for the second time, and Alfred, still unknown, was waiting for his first big chance in a New York lead. A young English actress (born in Woodford) had come to stay with them; a quiet girl for whom a few stray prophecies had indeed foretold a possible future whenever she was seen patiently waiting outside managerial offices for brief and often discouraging interviews. "She's not good-looking," they said —a statement which has since become a first-class joke— "but there's something *in* her!"

To Lynn's surprise, Alfred and his mother frequently went out alone into the garden, pacing up and down in heavy conference over the acute financial situation, no money even to pay for his ticket to New York. They decided to put on a Variety Show for Genesee; a program was hastily thrown together: Alfred, Lynn, Karen, Louise, a friend who sang songs at the piano, dances, recitations, comic turns. Confidently they rehearsed, and expected an enormous crowd to replenish the empty exchequer. But when the night came, it brought the worst heat-wave that had been known for years; twelve gallant people struggled through the blazing, sweaty weather, and the show went on—leaving the company thirty dollars in the red.

*   *   *   *

I have a mental collection of moments on the stage, of horror, irony, beauty or tension ("Memorabilia"); and once, over twenty years ago, I wrote them down, more to remind myself than benefit my readers, because such collections are a very individual affair. Until I looked it up, I thought I had not included any thrilling "moment" supplied by the Lunts, because I had not yet seen them on the stage . . . but then I turned a page and memory quickened and came alive: The style, the *panache* and suddenness with which Alfred leapt over the sofa at the end of that love-scene played on a narrow tight-rope in *Design for Living*:

> OTTO: What small perverse meanness in you forbids you to walk round the sofa to me?
>
> GILDA: I couldn't move if the house was on fire!
>
> OTTO: I believe it is. To hell with the sofa! (He vaults over it and takes her into his arms. They stand holding each other closely and gradually subside on to the sofa.)
>
> OTTO (kissing her): Hvordan star det til!
>
> GILDA (blissfully): What's that, darling?
>
> OTTO: "How do you do?" in Norwegian.
>
> THE CURTAIN SLOWLY FALLS

But that, as I said, was twenty years ago. What further moments can I pick out and offer you from magical hours at *The Guardsman, Reunion in Vienna, Idiot's Delight, Amphitryon 38, The Taming of the Shrew, There Shall Be No Night, Love in Idleness* or *Quadrille?*

Here is Lynn, in a scene of *Quadrille*, conveying without a word that after years of restraint, her heart has run away with her head and she is on the verge of following it. Every gesture demonstrates her uncontrollable happiness; a hurdy-gurdy starts to play in the street, and "Serena" begins to waltz round the room; she is young again, she is loved again, and she couldn't care less about what she is leaving behind!

"Alfred Lunt's back" . . . Have I indeed heard the announcement on the Home Service of the B.B.C., during a spirited session of "Twenty Questions"—"Our next object is abstract with strong animal attachments"? . . . Yet not only his eloquent back, but the nape of his neck, the curve of his shoulder, are perpetually and to a startling degree significant of what may be going on in his mind. In *Quadrille* he was cast as a rich railway magnate, a business man in the Middle West in the 1870's, as it might have been his father, his grandfather, his uncles; he revelled in the rôle with atavistic delight, and told me that for him it was not acting at all; for at every performance more and more came back to him of how they moved, what words they would have stressed, how they would have *thought* in order to produce just that movement and that stress. . . .

And never in recent years have I been so convinced that the hero and heroine of a play were bound to live happy ever after, as when in that final courteous moment of *Quadrille*, having finished their breakfast coffee at the

Boulogne station buffet, and with the bell clanging for the departure of the Paris-Lyons-Méditerranée express, Axel offers Serena his arm and they go out together; not self-conscious romantics, not defying the conventional world, but conveying by their walk, the carriage of their heads, the very way that in passing he picks up his grey top-hat from the table and puts it on, a serene certainty that all will be well.

Lynn is undoubtedly beautiful when cast for a part where she is young and gay, yet I am inclined to think her exquisite bone formation shows forth best when she is sorrowful and suffering and "looks her age." (It is odd how women as well as men worship her looks without a trace of the jealousy such enchantment usually calls forth, but as though they were grateful to her for giving her whole sex a boost.) Such poignant beauty, I remember, stayed with her during the last brief scene of *There Shall Be No Night*, in choosing presently to face the victorious enemy's fire rather than give in. In a previous scene, her husband, a scholar of note, left alone in the deserted schoolroom which had been army headquarters, picked up his revolver, holding it awkwardly in a way which we knew must prove useless, and looking at a heroic quotation (from Euripides, I think) painted round the walls, moved out quietly, without an exit line, to where his men were already engaged in a last hopeless stand. I do include in my collection of memorabilia that silent moment of clumsiness with his weapon, yet find it difficult to isolate from the whole of *There Shall Be No Night* which, although tragic, failed to harrow us like certain other great tragedies; for I postulate that dividing our emotional reactions into sad on one side and harrowed on the other, is not merely arbitrary: we are devastated as well as

heartbroken by *King Lear* because the leading protagonist, humanly speaking has ignobly brought it all on
himself; whereas after *There Shall Be No Night*, we quit
the theater with the ultimate satisfaction of recognizing
that the couple whose country was invaded during the last
World War, were inspired by an unfaltering instinct to
behave so as to cast no discredit on mankind facing a
crisis. The bad behavior of our fellow-creatures in real
life always has to be viewed with the tolerance engendered
by our own potentialities to lapse into similar failure under stress; yet I maintain (in vigorous argument) that I
am willing to grant myself capable of anything ... except
the rotten psychology of Lear in judging his two elder
daughters and misjudging the younger, in spite of those
many years he must have spent in their company, solely
by the way Goneril and Regan laid it on with a trowel,
and Cordelia, fed up by the grossness of their flattery,
went a little far towards the other extreme of delicate
restraint. However, that is matter for an essay—(the argument, I remember, became too heated to have any further
value, when it led us via *Hamlet* and *Macbeth* into
Othello). Besides, I want to put on record Alfred Lunt's
interpretation of Petruchio. *The Taming of the Shrew*,
being a rampageous comedy-farce, absolves us from a
moral need to "make allowances" for Petruchio's methods of taming; but when Alfred played the part, by
another silent revealing moment that I shall never forget,
he let us in on the man's deep reluctance to assume such
brutal insensitivity: it happened at the end of one of those
mannerless brawls between the pair, where one might
have assumed (and perhaps Shakespeare meant us to assume) that the bully only cared about getting his way
by shouting and stamping like a madman; but after Kate

the Shrew had swept off, crying from thwarted rage
at having met her master, Petruchio suddenly collapsed
from sheer weariness and leaned exhausted against the
door ... by his complete surrender conveying how hate-
fully the masquerade had gone against the grain, and that
he loved Kate, really loved her, but in carrying on in
this abominable fashion until she capitulated lay their only
hope of ultimate happiness.

I possess four photographs of the Lunts, two professional, and two which show them not acting at all, but
affectionately wanting their frends to have a glimpse of
them as they paused for a moment in their daily life at
home in Genesee, Wisconsin: picnicking under a haycock
in the blazing sun (to judge from Alfred's hat); a rough-
and-ready picnic, nothing luxuriously supplied: I should
call it, in fact, a quick meal being cooked by Alfred with
Lynn amused though a little critical, and Alfred just *not*
saying "All right, do it yourself!" because he is unwilling
to yield the saucepan. And in the last of these spontaneous
reproductions of moments in their life at home in Genesee,
we cannot even deduce from their faces what is going on;
they are in their gardening clothes—not stage gardening
clothes, but the sloppy, unattractive kind really worn
while on the job, and their backs are turned to us as they
tramp off down the path presumably leading to Ten
Chimneys, each carrying a load fairly enough divided between male and female.

I had, in pre-war days, heard much of this house at
Genesee, and was warmly invited to visit them, though
Alfred's inducements were mainly culinary, not architectural. His passionate hobby—and probably at moments
the salvation of his reason—is cooking. Lynn cooks too,
and "too" is not meant in disparagement, for I gather that

her experiments are always successful, Alfred's only sometimes; but his are less casually undertaken: he is a chef
with a chef's grave respect for the exact science, while
she will say at rare intervals: "I think I'll make an English fruit-cake," and presently will appear with a perfect
English fruit-cake. So you can imagine how dismayed I
felt, looking forward to long hours spent in the company
of this glamorous pair in their own home, on receiving
Alfred's serious assurance, from motives of the purest consideration for a-writer's-work-never-done, that I need not
see them at all the whole time I was there: trays would
be left outside my door, and trays fetched away again
when I had honored them by my solitary eating on the
premises what they had so lovingly prepared for me.
"That *would* be fun!" I remarked sardonically; but their
genuine humility interfering for once with their sense of
humor, I believe they saw nothing amiss with the program.

DAVID LLOYD GEORGE

HERO-WORSHIP, unlike fairy-tale endings, will never have a door slammed in its face; and if real life does not oblige for the moment with a live hero, biographies will supply him. The study of a man's life, his unconscious demonstration of what can be done from start to finish, has a steadying effect on us, like keeping a hand on a rope alongside when crossing a precipice. Men and women who evoke romantic hero-worship apart from their direct achievements usually have a potent quality of generous vitality. Churchill has it, with a rare force of personal impact; Francis of Assisi had it, and Roosevelt and Nelson and Robert Louis Stevenson and David Lloyd George.

I first met Lloyd George in the early 1930's; he was a splendid-looking old man, as vital and entertaining at breakfast as at dinner. I can still hear him describing the Welsh preachers with flowing white beards and bare feet, who used to stride down the hill into the village street when he was a small boy, and gather crowds around them, urchins and veterans offering themselves to this tremendous eloquence. And here Lloyd George's blue eyes would flash bluer, and his silver hair seem to blaze and crackle round his head, and his voice ring out with the same vibrant note as the preachers who years before must have held the little impressionable youngster spell-bound; while his forefinger emphasized one of their parables, his favorite, of a pilot on the Sea of Galilee during a raging storm: Three times he refused to turn and go back to shore—"And if we sink, *the bows will still be towards Galilee.*" Lloyd George swore that his whole life, as well as his oratory, was built on the memory of these ancient preachers. And looking at him then, I was easily moved to believe that their spirit could have passed into our Prime Minister during the early period of the 1914 war; the losing period. *And if we sink—*

Here in his own house at Churt, Bron-y-de, Gaelic for Breast of the South (even though it faces north; a perpetual twinkling joke against whoever had been responsible), the dining-room chairs and table were hand-made in oak from the estate, every chair equally comfortable with broad arm-rests, not only for those at the top and bottom; because Lloyd George, though an autocrat, was fundamentally aware of good hostmanship. And here he related how Jellicoe, Maurice Hankey and Winston Churchill gathered informally round his breakfast-table in Downing Street, used to discuss and decide with him what was to be done during that black, hopeless time when the tonnage of the shipping losses was heavier every day: "Och, it was dreadful. Every morning when we came down, the first thing we saw was the loss in tonnage. . . . And it seemed there was nothing we could do to stop it. Jellicoe said he *couldn't* stop it. And then I decided to try convoys. He said they'd never keep pace. But they kept pace beautifully. I remember at Boulogne, seeing the long line of little steamers and the torpedo-boat leading them. And so we got him round, at breakfast, to say 'Yes.' I said we *had* to have them. If they rammed each other, which was the worst that could happen, we'd be no worse off than now. But Jellicoe was too clever a man—you *knew* when he was wrong, but he could put it so cleverly that you couldn't get at him. I'd always far rather have a stupid man at the head of affairs at a time like that. All these old sea-admirals brought up in the tradition, they wouldn't listen when younger men came to them with ideas; they resented it: 'What, teach *us*? Men who've been in the Service for forty, fifty years, to be taught their business by a *middy*?' And the 'middies' got a black mark for even bringing along their ideas. But I encouraged them; and so we got the paravane—a device that's pushed in front of ships to explode a mine prematurely, and the hydrophone by which one can listen for the enemy submarine *through* the water, and then throw your mine and shake its plates to make them come loose. And the method of smearing ships with saccharin, so that they and the whole water were suddenly picked out with fire, white and luminous and brilliant, and you could easily see the periscopes of submarines sticking up out of the water on a moonless night. Once Winston and I landed from Boulogne after a miserable visit to France; and we saw the little Celties of eighteen marching out, the last to be called up, about five feet four; and suddenly out came the white fire all over the black water. And another idea, eight tall concrete towers we'd have planted across the Channel to make a bridge with nets between to catch . . . bad fish; only the war ended before they were ready. You can still see one of them at Shoreham.

"I don't think anyone realizes on how few brains we won the war. The attics—you know what I mean?—the men at the top—they were our weak point. Ah, but luckily they were the weak point on the other side, too. Look at the Kaiser, led by vanity, vanity all the way; and if it hadn't been for Bethmann von Holweg's liver. . . . The Germans were simply waiting and waiting for orders to march on Paris in 1914, but they had no one at the top to give orders; the finest army of men and officers that ever took the field. I'm a Celt—'superstitious' if you must put a name to what I'd call a miracle of God in March, 1918; they broke the gap in the English-French front and could have marched through and on to Amiens—and they didn't. Ludwig told me it was because there was a snowstorm which caked the wheels of the ammunition-carriages. 'Why didn't you move *after* the snowstorm?' 'A sudden outbreak of Spanish 'flu,' he said, the plague, Providence. . . . *And who's behind a snowstorm and Providence*, tell me that?

"I sent right round every Front to try and find one of the younger generals to justify giving him the General Command at that desperate stage of affairs. What a chance missed for a youngster! But there wasn't one, not one. So I insisted on Foch having it. '*A Frenchman?*' everyone squealed, 'set over *us?*' As if that was a time for patriotic indignation. It didn't matter a damn if he could do the trick. Luckily Haig agreed, otherwise . . . we'd have been lost.

"When I asked Ludwig about von Mackensen, the answer was: 'Puss-in-Boots.'

"But you're not eating? Don't you like my honey? We

make our own bread. We could stand a siege here. I wonder, will Bron-y-de ever be besieged?"

And he boasted that his guests who breakfasted with him were given Bron-y-de honey, Bron-y-de eggs, rich yellow butter and cream and home-made bread, jam from that year's ripe gooseberries, and apples from his orchards; and that he gave a lunch-party at which only his own produce had been served, and Keynes had passed a motion that his brawn should be subsidized but his raspberry wine prohibited. I myself can testify that his heather mead was hardly a drink for the gods, unless, maybe, the gods of Valhalla.

In front of the house a heather garden, purple and red and white, richly attracted the bees. Lloyd George surveyed them proudly as they glutted themselves on what he had provided. He was like an old god of fecundity, his brain teeming with plans of perpetual increase, yet already his orchards doubled the blossom and fruit of any other man, and his hens, his ducks, his turkeys and geese gave birth to twice as many young; they dared not do less! He could not bear slowness. I have heard him rage with impatience on the telephone.

Philip Snowden was his nearest neighbor anad friend; that delicate, lame man with his clear-cut pallor, his integrity of frost and ice, and the rare smile, sweeter than I have ever seen on the face of any politician. Though they were not of the same party, Lloyd George felt towards him the protective affection of a strong, older brother who did not know himself what illness was. When Snowden broke down from over-work and nearly died, during his long painful convalescence Lloyd George used to send in literally the cream of his dairy produce every day; and he related with delight that on Snowden's first reappearance in the House, he smiled as he limped past and whispered: "*Your* cream did this."

Ll. G. had a great affection for Winston Churchill, too, and was for ever talking about him. He believed that politics were more loyal than people always supposed, and not nearly as corrupt: "But you should keep in the same place, and then your constituents will learn that they can trust you." In a speech at a Zionist meeting he threw out: "Your three great Jews, Moses, Isaiah, and Jesus," expecting them to flinch at the third name—"And they did! They did!" Furthermore, he said, Christ was "not a man who noticed His surroundings or cared for practical comfort and luxuries; He had a culture and a fineness above all that."

As for reading, Wild West stories competed with historical novels, provided they had happy endings; D'Artagnan and Alan Breck were his heroes; braggarts who justified their vanity and were really brave men.

He asked me, laughing, who was the greatest bragger on earth. And answered his own question: "A landowner showing his friends round." Of the thieving birds he said: "Let them eat. I'm willing to pay for my orchestra." He spoke of himself as "the old grey fox whom they can't catch in a trap"; and he discoursed as a professional farmer on wire-worm, the cabbages, and the rooks. Then again, his thoughts back on politics, he mentioned the Dole: "It's a water-cart to lay the dust; when the dust rises, you get the Revolution." His tastes were for buttermilk, Rhine wines and champagne, and Pilsener beer at the end of a walk. His own bedroom at Bron-y-de was a different version of butter-milk: an innocent room with pale walls; a single chest of drawers in his own holly wood; sepias, very tender and sweet, of Welsh mountain scenery. But in the most sumptuous of the spare rooms stood a screen of sea-waves worked in blue silk, a present sent to him by the old Mikado as an offering after the first World War. On a desk in this room stood an inkstand inscribed to the effect that it was made of the hoof of the cow which had kicked Mr. Gladstone in—(I forget which year)—and "presented to David Lloyd George by his loyal constituents."

We visited the small chickens, and the new cherry orchard on vast fields of brown earth which he had just reclaimed from wasteland; in a wood farther off, yesterday's bonfire was still smouldering under its ashes; so we set it roaring again, Lloyd George dragging up a wheelbarrow with loads of brushwood and heather and bundles of sticks, throwing them on recklessly to feed the flames, gleeful as any boy on Guy Fawkes day. He chose a stick for my collection, that time or another time, from the nut-hedge bordering one of the fields: "I can't cut it for you now with the sap rising, but it's a good one, straight and strong," and knotted his colored handkerchief round it, so that he should recognize it in the autumn. He was quite right, it *is* a good walking-stick, and I still use it more than any other; on the silver band he put the inscription: G.B.S. FROM BRON-Y-DE. Ll.G., and I felt it to be a stick with virtue in it.

One night he chose to retire to bed early, and made a solemn, statesmanlike departure at 10:05 p.m., overburdened with piles of manuscript, reference books, files and so forth, for the last volume of his *War Memoirs*. He even sent Frances for several more books that had been forgotten. We were deeply impressed, and stood talking of him for a few moments in the shadowy room, after we had turned out the lights, meaning almost at once to fol-

low his example and go to our beds. Indeed, he thought
we had, for presently we heard stealthy footsteps . . . and
not seeing we were still there, he entered and tiptoed
across to fetch a cheap edition of a Zane Grey Wild West
story-book which he had inadvertently left lying on the
bench in front of the fire. Then he caught sight of a bottle
of lollipops known as "satin cushions," picked out one
with care, a yellow one, and with his cheek bulging, tiptoed away again.

Undoubtedly the Wild West beckoned him with its
adventurous schoolboy lure. Nearly every evening while
I stayed at Bron-y-de, and especially if we were alone,
he and Frances and I, he would insist that this own private
little cinema should present a selection from an ancient
library of films, most of them old-fashioned Westerns,
cracked and flickering. Wearing a no less ancient mole-
colored velvet coat and waistcoat, he sat between us on
the couch, absorbed and entirely happy at seeing cowboys
plunge down into the ravine and ride straight up the wall
of the precipice on the further side in pursuit of the
Wicked Sheriff who had carried off Brave Bessie the
Good Sheriff's daughter. Yes, he approved of cowboys,
and disliked elegant people who cut snippets off pears
and apples and ate them with a knife and fork instead of
boldly burying their faces in the fruit.

Frances and I and, I think, Sir William Beveridge dined
with him in his London flat on the night when he had
consented to speak on the radio for the first time. He left
us there to listen in, when he went off with many misgivings to fulfill his engagement at the B.B.C. It was the
only time I saw Lloyd George not fully confident of his
powers; and indeed he was justified, for none of his usual
fire and magnetism came across. He spoke on a low drag-

ging note, except once when mysteriously his voice leapt up, rapid and jovial . . . then presently subsided again. When he returned, anxiously asking: "How was I?" (but already knowing the answer) he told us that the sudden change was the result of a card being thrust in front of him while he was at the mike, with the admonition "Too sad" written on it. He explained that he had to *see* his audience of men and women, feel their antagonism or enthusiasm, and that a little room with dead walls and an unresponsive disc was of no use to him at all. He would have been marvellous on television, for with a human audience he had a chance; he could intoxicate them by his oratory, but only if they could see as well as hear him, and if he too could see them respond.

And that was entirely true. The only time I had the good fortune to hear him speak in public was in 1932, at the National Liberal Club, when he had just returned from a voyage to Ceylon, following his long, dangerous illness of the previous year.

All his enemies had foretold that he was finished, done for; that his day was over and it were better he had not attempted this theatrical sort of resurrection. His friends did not phrase it like that, but they too were apprehensive that the fires had guttered down. Therefore friends and enemies were gathered there, but only the latter expected to triumph. Lloyd George moved slowly on to the platform with bowed shoulders, leaning heavily on the arm of his chairman; he sank down as though exhausted even from that brief journey; and when he rose to deliver his speech after the introduction, he could still hardly stand upright, his very hairs seemed limp, his eyes downcast, his voice feeble and quavering. Our hearts sank, and his opponents exchanged glances as he referred timidly to his astonishment that they should still care to come and hear him, an old man, recently he had thought a dying man. . . .

Wily old man! For after these first few halting sentences, he suddenly flung off his disguise and regained his potency. The effect was terrific, not only of his voice, but of his whole appearance when he sloughed his disguise as an actor throws off a cloak. Half an hour later he was still thundering on with no trace of fatigue, and friend and foe, responding with cheers and laughter and stamping feet, were metaphorically clambering over each others' shoulders and swinging from the staircase and gallery, signalling exultant messages to the world: *"It's all right; he's in form again!"*

I should like to have heard Demosthenes and Burke and Disraeli and all the others. They die and are lost, and modern science can only preserve their voices, not their magnetic influence.

What a Welshman he was! We never had cowboy films on the nights when there was a program of Welsh singers or Welsh speakers or a Welsh religious festival, for he would not miss any of these. He used a Welsh shepherd's crook, and reported gleefully the success of newspapers printed in Welsh. Nor was he ever afraid of appearing in picturesque clothes, which by a lucky chance were also the most comfortable: a grey-blue suit, incredibly old, a faded green cloak draped in lavish Tennysonian folds about his broad person, and an incredibly battered greyish-green hat slouched on his brilliant silver hair. Thus attired, he set out for our daily walk round the estate; little Jennifer, in her blue cloth coat and little blue velvet cap, insisted on carrying a stick too; he called her *Cariad*, Welsh for darling.

A small sapling beech tree grew in the middle of his

lawn; and he told me he had said when he planted it: "If it survives, so will the Liberal Party."

It did survive, but has been cut down since his death.

Ll.G. loved trees. In his library he stuck a branch of silver birch-tree in young leaf into a jar, and was sad when it had to be thrown away.

PAMELA FRANKAU

I HOPE I may not sound unduly pompous if I start this personal portrait by an Enquiry into the Nature of Autobiography, and some Asides on the Further Device of Fiction as a supplement; plus evidence inadvertently supplied by the extrovert and withheld by the introvert. A born introvert renders it unnecessary to re-read her autobiography for clues, because if we try to extract more from it than the already generous allowance she has chosen to give, we are guilty of a violation of privacy; while with an extrovert it would be superfluous to re-read it; which need not denote perpetual tiresome chatter from a shallow egoist, but an unreserved disposition, who flings you presents the whole time you are together, and all you have to do is thankfully pick them up and fit them into their proper place. Thus I made no search for forgotten treasure in *I Find Four People* by Pamela Frankau (the autobiography of an extrovert), except to flick through the pages backwards from the end to the beginning and refresh my memory on her attitude to her well-known parent, Gilbert Frankau. Not that I can include his importance on her psyche in the half-dozen variations of "Life with Father" which I have already mentioned, for he nonchalantly strolled out of her existence in her early childhood, and only rejoined it after some fourteen years of indifference on either side.

There is a device less exact and formal than biography by which we may if we choose (and if they choose) introduce you to an intimate friend: in 1932 I wrote a light novel called *Long Lost Father*, in which Carl Bellairs, who ran the fashionable Tipstaff restaurant, was played by John Barrymore in a Hollywood film version; a letter I possess from that now legendary idol of the American stage ends on a postscript: "My manager has this moment told me that *Long Lost Father* is crystallized. Thank the Lord!" . . . "This moment" makes 1933 look poignantly far away from 1958.

Long Lost Father could in no way be called a *roman à clef* featuring the family life of the Frankaus: "Lindsay Bellairs," a young cabaret singer, Carl's only child, I described as fair and audacious, on excellent terms with a step-father whose understanding, generosity and tact, combined with a real talent for non-interference, may perhaps be a pendant to Pamela's own step-mother in real life, Susan Frankau. Otherwise, Pamela herself has short dark hair and toffee-colored eyes (her own unflattering description), and is not an only child but (literally) blessed with an elder sister, Ursula; she has never sung in cabaret nor (if we can prevent it) anywhere else; and as nobody could pretend that the original of Peter Jackson, Cigar Merchant, was a middle-aged philanderer who achieved notoriety as an urbane *maître d' hotel* in the most

exclusive restaurant of London's West End, it will be
seen that *Long Lost Father* was solely recognizable by its
situation of a young daughter casually reunited with her
father, after her subconscious had been indignant for
eighteen years at the slight put upon her mother by his
absence; a crusade which meanwhile had made her judge
him severely, for her friendship with her mother was one
of the main planks of her life; she admits in her autobiography that it was only many years later, at war's end in
1945, that "a sequence of outrageous battles" also brought
their personal peace-treaty. And apart from the respect
he awoke in her by his invariable self-discipline towards
the claims of work, and a disarming capacity to "ruffle
well" in a fight, love did not spring into green leaf between
them until the last years of his life.

My fictional version of the Daddy theme, therefore was,
mainly based on a belated awakening (twice) of Carl's
age-long instinct to wreck a possible companionship as
of one human being to another, by exercise of paternal
discipline at the wrong moment:

> Something had happened to him; it was the germ of
> being a father. A germ totally new to Carl. He had no
> idea, of course, how powerful it was, and yet how in-
> sidious, once it pervaded the system . . . He did not
> know its potentialities.

According to Pamela, one of the things Gilbert had
actually said during this thundering row, was "I've heard
enough of your worthless friends"—and from a sudden
halt in her reminiscences and lame recovery, I believe I
must have been included among them. Furthermore he
remarked: "If you would only put your intelligence into

your life and your emotions into your books instead of vice versa, you'd die a very rich woman."

The other day, an older, wiser Pamela took stock with me of her Matchgirl phase. "Matchgirl" was my own name for her, from the story by Hans Christian Andersen, and suggested by her condition of permanent and spectacular insolvency . . . There she sat, half-frozen, on the snowy doorstep of the big house, offering her matches; inside were feasting and merriment and all the lights blazing on the Christmas tree; but the poor little matchgirl had not sold a box all day . . . Pamela was always more uninhibited about her poverty-stricken state than anyone I have ever known; and still from old habit she absently signs her letters *Matchgirl* when she writes to me, even during her Croesus periods. In the three years following publication of her first novel, *Marriage of Harlequin*, she *was* Croesus; or to vary the classical analogy, a youthful Midas; everything she touched turned to gold, and magazines paid her fantastic prices for short stories. Then came the lean years; authorship is, let's face it, a capricious profession! Here was a father's chance; he banished her to a picturesque village in the Cotswolds, Shipton-under-Wychwood, where (he decreed sternly) she was to work and write and finish her novel *Tassell-Gentle*; work and write and sleep, and for recreation take a nice healthy walk. And she was to be *alone*: no visitors, no drink, no money; the hotel would send him her bills and he would settle them. Drastic treatment for a rake, and Young Pamela *was* a rake . . . I remember a certain dinner at the Ivy when she had been lit and gay and irrepressible and more than somewhat foolish; I desired to indicate, therefore, when I greeted her coldly across the restaurant at lunchtime the next day, that I had no further interest in her extravagant capers. Astonished at my manner, she came over and badgered me to tell her what was wrong? When I told her—"Aren't you being rather *grown-up?*" she demanded, disappointed in me. But these moments were bound to occur between us, for Pamela having her fling was (and still is) seventeen years my junior; a difference in age far less noticeable now in the nineteen-fifties than in the nineteen-thirties when our first meeting took place under the protective aegis of one of the great hostesses of the period: my dear friend Eliza Aria, Frank Danby's sister, Gilbert Frankau's Aunt Eliza, Pamela's great-aunt. I must turn again to *I Find Four People* for her impressions of celebrities she met through Aunt Eliza: Michael Arlen, Sybil Thorndike, Osbert Sitwell, John van Druten, Rebecca West, Margaret Irwin, H. G. Wells . . . Later, most of us were to burst the age barrier and be treated as her contemporaries, with happy affection. These first few encounters, however, were all awe and seeing-Shelley-plain. G. B. Stern figures as perhaps the least interesting; a personage of elderly benevolence, contemporary of Great-Aunt Eliza's, with silvery hair, ivory and ebony cane, and a careless pat on the shoulder when addressing the timid, ambitious child.

Nowadays, with the same religion, the same profession, the same sense of proportion as to what is and is not essential, the same occasional nonagenarian lapses in health and vitality owing to our great age, the chief visible incompatibility shows in her capacity still to stay up (if and when required) until well beyond midnight without wondering if the skies are going to fall; whereas I have never displayed any talent for sitting up late, and was always amazed at my friends who could let ten p.m. move on into eleven and twelve o'clock, and yet deplorably give

no sign of departure. I once invited three of them to dinner, and then had a brilliant idea and told Young Pamela
she could come too as an education . . . and as a useful
means of getting rid of my other guests at a seemly hour:
I gave her clear instructions, and she listened big-eyed,
intimidated by the prospect of this ripe, sophisticated trio
of worldlings, Lady Colefax and Sidney Dark and Louis
Bromfield; famous hostess and famous Editor and famous
novelist. They seemed a bit surprised at her presence,
called her "Dear," and otherwise took no notice of her—
except to keep scandal within bounds as we sat talking
round the fire after dinner while Sidney poured out huge
tulip-glasses filled (to the brim) with old Napoleon
brandy for himself and Louis, and at intervals refilled
them (to the brim) without looking what he was doing;
it had been offered to "the ladies" and refused, but not,
of course, to the little girl sitting deferential and silent on
a hassock—or at any rate giving an impression of sitting
on a hassock; the deferential part of it was genuine. Only
she happened to like Napoleon brandy, while Sidney
Dark no doubt thought she would have called it "horrid
stuff—it burns my throat—" and ask for crème de menthe
instead. The clock struck ten, very near my moment of
release, for at twenty past, if nobody had departed yet,
Pamela was due to spring up and do her act and thus
put the idea into their heads and set goodbyes in motion:
"Good Lord, I'd no idea it was so late—" etc., fulsomely
apologetic for having kept me up. But at twenty past,
damn it, Young Pamela hadn't budged! I looked at her
meaningly. Another ten minutes . . . and galvanized by
my unspoken terrorism, she scrambled to her feet: "Well,
I must be going now. Thank you for a lovely evening."
Never before nor after have I heard her speak her lines

so unconvincingly. The pundits nodded their goodnights, obviously relieved at the prospect of the child's departure. With the impediment to grown-up conversation now removed, they thankfully relaxed and settled down to telling those luscious scandals which until now they had bowdlerised or kept back altogether for fear of shocking my mute and doubtless innocent little niece or whatever she was; while Young Pamela went swaggering along to a really riotous, dissolute, debauched orgy that wouldn't end till past three a.m.

"And a fat lot of use *you* were!" I flung at her in the hall. And only anxious to oblige, she asked "Do you want me to go back and do it again? I will if you like."

During the nineteen-thirties we knocked around together a good bit, not only in England but at Sligachan on Skye, in a harmonious quartet with John van Druten and Jack Cohen; Pamela's vivid yet dreamlike description of Skye, in *I Find Four People*, lets me off from vain striving to make readers see it through my eyes; they can see it through hers; unlike Henry V, I am not covetous for honor. On another expedition, after mooching contentedly round Salisbury Cathedral and the Close and surrounding water-meadows, Pamela and I stopped on our way home at an Inn near Oxford, where we spent the night in a thick fog as guests of T. H. White, who had just roused all of us to a great burst of admiration for his beautiful comical Arthurian fantasy *The Sword in the Stone*—(" 'Come along, Robin Hood,' snapped King Pellinore, for once in a temper, 'stop leaning on your bow *with that look of negligent woodcraft*' ")—But here again, in spite of several Stingers hopefully poured down my throat, I soon lapsed from coeval sympathy into being a cross old veteran wanting her bed, while Pamela the Rake sat up enthralled by his company, drinking and talking, talking and drinking, until the dawn. In self-defense, however, I discovered a day later that I was very ill— doctor-ill, day-and-night-nurse-ill—so perhaps there was some excuse for my anti-social mood.

And there were two or three summer house-parties at the Villa Mysto near Anthéor in the South of France; a pattern of memories in drowsy blue and gold. Our days were spent bathing in the Mediterranean, and then lying in the sun or shade according to physical preference; reluctantly going apart to write—(four out of five of us wrote for a living)—and assembling again for paradisaical meals by Cecile who cooked passionately, her fiery soul usefully stirred into the sauces and seasonings; if she thought that too much of any voluptuous dish was sent out again, she rushed from the kitchen into the *salle à manger* prostrating herself in despair, volubly demanding wherein she had failed? An existence which I still think could not have been bettered; lovely, aromatic honey smells came into it, and the song of nightingales and so forth. Dancing? Gambling? Nowadays at the barest mention of the tables at Monte Carlo, Pamela's eyes get that glazed, insane, can't-stay-away look; but needing then no set entertainment, we all entertained one another, ate *canelotti*, fresh sardines, *beignets de courgettes* and every romantic variation on the theme of salad and soufflé, drank *vin du pays*, slept deeply and well, and cared not when Cecile's husband, the local postman, brought us no letters; in this self-contained Eden, what did we want with letters from beyond?

It was there that I wrote my first and last whodunit— about a house-party in a villa on the Mediterranean, and one of them gets murdered, and the survivors were suspected of the murder. It proved not a bad thriller; reviewing it for, I think, the *Tatler*, Evelyn Waugh advised firmly that I should stop writing those tiresome old family chronicles, the Rakonitzes and so forth, and devote my talents, such as they were, entirely to thrillers. I used the house-party's real names, and altered them only in the final version I sent up to the publishers. My secretary drew a map of the downstairs and upstairs of the villa as a frontis-piece, but forgot to alter just one name . . . Throughout the book, Pamela was "Prunella"; but in England and the U.S.A., clearly printed and an essential feature of the plot. Prunella's bedroom has been immortalized in the map as *"Pamela's* bedroom" . . . and thus it stands for ever and ever. "Not every maiden keeps her r-r-room so neat!" remarked Beerbohm Tree as Mephisto looking in at the window of Gretchen's maidenly bower; a caption for *Pamela's bedroom* which she has found difficult to live down.

In January 1940, Pamela and I were forced apart by circumstances well beyond our control: I was in a nursing-home, having septicaemia and major operations; Pamela, after the worst blow of her life, was going haywire in the States. And though we did not know it, that was goodbye to Young Pamela.

In the early summer of 1941, she and I met again, and for a brief hour recaptured nonsense. My home in London had been wiped out by an incendiary bomb; and still a bit shaky and privileged and convalescent, I was inhabiting a furnished cottage at Aston Tirrold in Berkshire; and for the first time of the year I had hauled out the striped canvas deck-chairs on to the lawn, and the bright cushions from the summerhouse. Silence and illness and the At-

lantic and tragedy and bombs and destruction, the surrender of France and the Battle of Britain, had widely
stretched between us; yet on the surface, despite Pamela's
A.T.S. uniform, normality had come back for a little
while. We both had so much talk bottled up and waiting
for this brief opportunity, that a whole day and another
day and another would not contain it: "*Now* . . . where
do we begin?"—The garden gate clicked and an old lady
trotted in carrying a small jar of marmalade and a card
case: "Miss Stern, you *must* forgive me for not having
called before! I've brought you—" She stayed an hour and
a half, gently gossiping. *That* was where we began. An
absurd incident, but we laughed so much that I think we
both only realized then how much we had missed the
striped deck-chairs on the lawn and all the apparatus of
light-hearted happiness.

Unlike sorrow, which allows itself to be described so
as to make the reader actually share the pain of it and
suffer vicariously, one's descriptions of light-hearted happiness rarely come off; they are apt to dwindle into anecdotes; and when someone writes you a letter enthusiastic-
ally describing a good time, you are often slightly irritated
because they have failed to draw you into the magic
circle; and wonder what this is all about, apt to think the
writer is being trivial, silly, hilarious over nothing at all.
A good time should be marked "perishable." So I have
brought in this tiny, brittle incident of the old lady and the
home-made marmalade, not to maintain that after all I *can*
describe nonsense and laughter, but on the contrary, that
they break and I can only politely hand you the pieces.
There are ten thousand such foolish stories in all our
lives. . . .

Pamela has a genius for slipping into nonsense; as also

with disconcerting suddenness and when least expected
or desired, she will become public-spirited. She has explained it on a confession of being secretly a coward
and finding an assumed truculence the most effective way
to deal with cowardice. I replied (if she let me reply?
—there's always a doubt!) that most of us are cowards;
I know I am: but, a braver fighter than I, she is unwilling
to let it go at that.

Since the war, and during those periods of missing her
during her long absences in America or France, I have
ceased to be single-minded about them, bowing my head
to the Inevitable. Wistfulness, in fact, is now dabbled
over with a coating of strong complaint. For she believes
in total disappearance without "keeping in touch" . . .
and meanwhile one is left with no idea where she is or
how long she may stay away or if things are going well
or ill with her. I had not heard from her for more than
six months; not even an inquiry for news at second-hand;
and there is something in me that cannot stay content with
"meanwhile" as a blank space. Does she imagine that when
she comes back she can pick up friendship with all its
delights exactly where she had left off? Yes, she does—
and can. So can I, but it required an effort to keep unspoken my justifiable reproaches. Until arguing one day
on the subject in "Woman's Hour" with Arnot Robertson ('It Depends What You Mean By Friendship') I let
it all rip, what I thought of a certain anonymous creature
and her pretty ways of independence. Suppose she had
needed me, in illness, say, or trouble or financial straits,
just as I am liable to need her? And it works the other
way round too: things, after all, must be happening to
both of us, all of us, nearly all the time. Keeping in touch
. . . Otherwise when we do meet again we have such an

enormous amount of leeway to make up; even the jokes get lost forever in that ocean of *meanwhile*.

Here Arnot Robertson, of the opposite School of Thought, informed me that my claims were "monstrous" and that *her* friends must always be free to come and go and do as they liked. I retorted that I had no intention of interfering with this over-rated freedom business, no "claims," no intention of "being possessive" or "demanding a regular correspondence"; all I wanted—I waxed eloquent and pathetic, complaining of Pamela to the women of Great Britain (except those who might have switched off) and I hoped someone would presently inform on me and tell her how I felt about my nameless, heartless friend. Someone presently did, and—"That's *me!*" she cried in high delight and no rancor. Certainly broadcasting can offer a new and luxurious opportunity to tell the world.

On her return she wrote me a very sweet if slightly puzzled letter of contrition, deploring an apparent neglect which had no bearing on her steady affection. Yet I doubt the contrition; we are as we are; and if I went off into the blue for months and years, it would never occur to Pamela and those of her School to notice that my life was elsewhere until regionally I returned to them again. She displayed more genuine remorse over an unimportant matter of losing a walking-stick which I had lent her when she had a strained back; months later, when her back was well and my fibrositis bad, I asked for its return because it happened to be the strongest in my collection; male malacca with an ivory handle ribbed underneath to take the grip of the fingers without slipping. I had given it to that fine painter, C. R. Nevinson, until he was tragically unable to walk at all any more; and he left instructions I was to have it again after he died. However, I had about forty-seven alternative walking-sticks, so there was no need for Pamela to carry on as though she had wilfully robbed me of my only babe and heir to the throne—"I'll get you the most expensive walking-stick money can buy," she promised passionately. Good! The *most* expensive that money could buy, doubtless designed by Fabergé or encrusted with jewels from a Maharajah's palace, would probably run her into several thousand pounds. If I mind excessively over what I think people *can* help, such as disinheriting me altogether from their concerns simply because I happen not to be there, I would never blame anyone for accidental losing or breaking; and in this case it was not Pamela but the removal van which was responsible, in transit with all her Lares and Penates to her first English home: a very charming little Victorian house bought with her friend Margaret Webster, the well-known theatrical producer, in a hilly part of old Hampstead village; Pamela's pride in it is good to see and (from my point of view) definitely reassuring as promising adieu to her nomad career; I am all for my close friends settling down within easy reach and not casting sheep's eyes any more in the direction of, say, Tierra del Fuego; and her new swagger over practical achievement such as cooking, appeared also to mark the end of Pamela the Rake with her wild parties and prodigal spending—"the approaching tide will shortly fill the reasonable shores." When both of us had solemnly vowed to pull in our horns—and not before pulling-in was overdue—we had a farewell dinner together at the Ivy, moderate in quantity but luscious in quality and expenditure, which by an historical association not quite clear to my ignorance ("Don't you mean Waterloo?") she persisted in calling our Eve of Quatre-bras.

I was amused a few months ago when a girl in her mid-twenties, after meeting her with me for the first time, remarked admiringly: "She was so tweedy and county, if you know what I mean?"—Pamela will always resemble a carven profile of Nefertiti, but "tweedy and county" showed her flesh and blood of that Gilbert Frankau who during an interlude in the early 1920's featured as Idol of the Cottesmore and Darling of the Quorn, riding furiously to hounds on his notorious yellow horse, Mustard-Pot! ("Did you hunt in pink, Gilbert?" I asked him when he had recovered from Shire-fever; and he replied with a grin: "I hunted in black and in terror, Peter!")

And on no later portrait of Pamela can I employ the words "assured" or "poised," without checking on a memory of an episode when the old diffidence, thrust away and out of sight, suddenly broke in and metaphorically thrust her back on to the hassock. An inferiority complex dies hard; Pamela's prevents her, for instance, from using clean towels laid out expressly for visitors in other people's bathrooms; she hunts round till she can find a towel sufficiently soiled to suit her lowliness; whereas I, packed close with wholly different brands of inferiority, nevertheless find no difficulty in using a clean towel as to the Manor born. A year or two ago, taking for granted that she was a Fellow of the Royal Society of Literature, I was puzzled at seeing her again overcome by one of these attacks.

"R. C. Sherriff is giving them a paper," I remarked, "and I've suggested he should have tea here first, so if you'd like to come along too, we could all go in your car. Who do you want to bring as your guest? Ursula?"

Followed a long silence.

"Of course I'll drive you there with pleasure," said

Pamela, her voice a little strained, "and wait outside."

"Wait *outside*?" Then light broke in. "Aren't you a Fellow of the R.S.L.?"

"I'm not nearly good enough," whispered the little Matchgirl.

"Nonsense," defending her status, "it's just that you slipped through the rungs, being in America for so many years." (And indeed, on later inquiry, that did account for it.) "Oh well, you can come as my guest in the meantime; and when it's over, we'll go on together to the Sheeds' cocktail party."

"Of course I'll drive you to the Sheeds too," said Pamela, becoming more lowly every moment.

"Pamela, what *is* all this humility about?" for her friendship with the Sheeds dated back further than mine. "They can't not have invited you?"

"They can't be expected to ask everybody to their party," bravely defending the Sheeds' refusal to keep open house to any sort of riff-raff like herself. She forbade me to ring up Frank Sheed, so naturally I did, directly I had got rid of her, and asked him whether Pamela had been invited?

Of course she had. Not likely that their dear Pamela would be left out.

"She thinks she hasn't been."

Frank went off immediately and made inquiries. He returned to the telephone shouting with laughter: "We split our invitation list and each took half, and Pamela was in my half and you in Maisie's. Maisie wrote all her cards and sent them off three days ago, but I haven't got down to mine yet."

To take stock of a friend's pilgrimage and progress from

watching her on T.V. is rather a modern form of assessment, like complaining of her on Radio; nor can I claim, since Pamela has not yet reached her fiftieth birthday, that I have beheld the "end-product." Nevertheless, it would be ungracious not to welcome the agreeable climate of her middle years. Lately I have seen her on a Brains Trust, and was amazed at her maturity and nous; not Young Pamela any more, nor the little Matchgirl, nor Pamela the Rake; not truculent because her inside reactions were shaky and precarious, but keeping her temper as it were without an effort, on a sense of humor and the consciousness of truth somewhere close at hand, and even if she should not be the one to voice it, ready to acknowledge its presence instead of proclaiming her subjective opinions at all costs. Television in some ways supplies us with the sort of portrait that we cannot see at the Royal Academy; nor on the stage, where though the characters are certainly three-dimensional, they speak parts written for them; while on the Brains Trust or any T.V. panel game you catch them unawares. She looked very juvenile and how-kind-of-you-to-let-me-join; and indeed, the rest of the team were charming to her without being patronizing, and ready on an instant to encourage her to speak; yet I felt that at any moment they might offer her a crème de menthe . . . Until out would come a piece of truth, quietly contributed, and she too is drinking old brandy.

When the Cenacle Convent in Hampstead held a Brains Trust "in the flesh," Pamela was again the youngest; I was able to sit at a stone's throw from five wise and witty members having their fling in a good cause, and watch her apparent spontaneity, half a speech thrown away as Gerald du Maurier threw away his speeches while strolling upstage; her gestures natural as though there were no audience—"Don't hit me!" an arm upraised after mischievously provoking the chairman's assumed wrath; more than once I was tempted to cry out with a great-aunt's pride: "*That's* my girl!" and privately wonder how she had arrived at such a finished technique. Or did I wonder? For she would explain—has indeed often and gratefully explained—that faith in herself, the small but precious quantity required, so to speak, to keep her going, had been engendered by a greater Faith in the Diety who fifteen years ago had moved in and taken possession, when a conventional Anglican upbringing, to be followed on religion's ever unpredictable curve by a phase of determined atheism, eventually brought an A.T.S. Officer Cadet in the O.C.T.U. at Edinburgh to the altar rail at Saint Columba's Roman Catholic Church.

And after God, or with Him, work is her Hound of Heaven: "I have a sense of guilt whenever I'm on holiday!" I should say she wrote from a deeper level than might be supposed from the light-hearted spirit in which I have described some of our personal encounters . . . As when Groucho's portrait, gorgeous and cocky, lay face uppermost on top of a pile of volumes in the Catholic bookshop, the natural idea would have been to assume that all the books underneath must perforce correspond with that initial impact. Her novels, though potential from the start, in my opinion began to be worth their salt only since the publication of *Shaken in the Wind;* at this juncture once again I let the dictionary pander to the lazy mind: *potential: existence in possibility not in act.* She has a rare talent, in her fiction, for reaching down to pain and suffering so that vicariously it hurts; and certain chapters in *The Bridge,* her latest novel, I should be reluctant to pick up and read again unless I could be sure I had time to go on to her triumphant-after-pain solution. There are two degrees of sophistication: the capacity to recognize

it as merely a halt at the frontiers for suffering, and a
cheap kind which travels no further, convinced that here
is the terminus. And having long ago impatiently discarded
any conventional happy-ever-after ending, she has more
lately discarded the modish style of happy-never-again,
in tacit acknowledgment of a strong prevailing need, as
yet unspoken, for something more spiritually *reasonable*;
disillusion must still exist, yet her adult sense of values
gives evidence that the ship need not sink when it reaches
the uncharted seas of despair, but can veer bravely in a
new direction. In *A Wreath for the Enemy*, the teen-age
heroine Penelope, daughter of an unconventional English
father running an hotel on the Riviera, yearns to belong
to an orthodox family who have taken the villa next door;
her forlorn awakening to their limitations when the other
two children desert her in a crisis and leave her to keep
vigil alone over the dead body of an eccentric, outrageous
old Duchess, might easily have proved wistfully sentimental in the style of those Victorian novelists, who
sought in vain to be "a potent force for good" ... but they
were not always blessed with Pamela's passionate sincerity,
and seldom with her gift for combining fundamentally religious with irresistibly funny.

"Irresistibly funny" leads me to give thanks for her entertainment value, nowadays more than ever appreciated
when one is perpetually brought down to desolation by
those clouds a great deal bigger than a man's hand passing
across the sun. Such as a brilliant imitation of herself as
Tyltyl in the school play; stepping before the curtain,
breathless and bashful and hitching her stockings to meet
the short *Lederhosen*, to speak the epilogue of Maeter-
linck's Blue Bird—"If any of you should find the Blue Bird,
will you please bring him back to us, because we shall need

him for our happiness later on!" And even more incongruous in a good-looking woman, responding to our request
to "make like Harpo"—and suddenly she *is* Harpo Marx,
a huge idiot grin mopping up half her face, eyes rolling
crazily round the room in search of a "skirt," and—such is
the force of suggestion—a rampageous mop of flaxen curls.
As for the quite unpublishable verses, rhymes and jingles
that she can rattle off impromptu at any moment, turn
and turn about with John van Druten, I can only look on
and envy them such a talent, at the drop of a hat to cause
us all to forget those pedestrian axioms that life is real,
life is earnest . . . Were I shipwrecked on a desert island
and given my choice of eight discs to be washed in from
the sea to keep me company, I would sacrifice the lot for
Pamela and Johnny, cross-talk comedians; "rather a fool
to make me merry than experience to make me sad."

Yet when our friends are unintentionally amusing they
must always endear themselves even more than by an entertainment purposely laid on . . . So I like to remember
Pamela looking for all the world like a wide-eyed little
boy with adenoids; lips parted, breathing heavy, incredulous gaze fixed on what the kind lady had just produced
from her cabinet of curios, carelessly remarking: "There
are a hundred ivory elephants in this bean!"—(the kind
lady was myself). *A hundred ivory elephants?* In one
small bean about the size of a thumbnail? Yes, it was true,
but I suppose I had taken them for granted since a friend,
a young airman, had brought me the bean from India; you
pull out the little stopper, and to convince the beholder,
shake out a few tiny elephants carved by Indian crafts-
men—how they ever found the time!—and when you have
about a dozen lying on your palm, start putting them back
for fear the whole hundred may tumble out and never be

fitted in again. "There you are," in matter-of-fact tones. But Pamela Frankau, distinguished novelist, continued in a silent trance, staring and staring, six years old, or at the most, seven!

None of these personal portraits is meant to be *revealing* of a whole life underneath; I have no right to reveal them, even where I can, whilst the subject is still alive to write or abstain from writing their own autobiography. Yet I appear to be focusing on Pamela alone this *apologia* for keeping well above the Plimsoll Line. Surmise and betrayal are insidious enemies to friendship, and flippancy a very natural safeguard; I make free, but I take care. We know that our friends are not "gratified" by excessive praise, but equally, when we speak of them (as I have done) affectionately, enjoying the fun of catching them unawares, they trust us not to lay bare those coverts which we have only entered by privilege.

And the closer they stand, the less simple does it become to present their story. Many of us have had experience of that sort of richly improbable autobiography which pours out of complete strangers who on very slight encouragement (or without) tell us the story of their life. But after their burst of uninhibited narrative, and if we do not part for ever but gradually along the years grow to know them well, the story of his or her life will reach a stage where it ceases to be coherent and consecutive . . . "*You can't see the wood for the trees!*" . . . In this volume, the intention is always towards a specific tree; the wood must take care of itself.

So I do not propose at this juncture to discourse at any length on the Works of Pamela Frankau, either from the reviewer angle, or as a pundit, defined by the dictionary as *learned creature*. Regular reviewers are not pundits; professionally employed to write on books and authors, they usually tackle the job with fairness and perception but not for pleasure (Marghanita Laski once likened it to Goblin Market); while a pundit (learned creature!) has no need to write on books and authors at all unless he has the urge and authority to express his view, using his mature judgment to right some tipsiness of balance or display the result of special research; *self-appointed* may be the key word. J. L. Furnas, one of the most companionable pundits to compel my respect and admiration, tried once to lure me into writing a monograph on a tramp who went about claiming to be the son of Robert Louis Stevenson; and incorporate therein a quantity of authentic information which happened to have reached me from voluntary sources as a result of a book I wrote whilst still thinking the tramp to be a legendary character. Replying to my objection that few people would be interested enough to read such a monograph, J. L. Furnas declared that that, so to speak, could not matter less; what mattered was that one more small section of hitherto uncharted territory in the biography of R.L.S. would thus have been dealt with, cleared up, and placed in safe keeping beyond mere conjecture. That is the true spirit of the pundit.

Yet you may well ask how this sudden spate of definition can have concern with my personal portrait of Pamela Frankau, penalizing her for being the most intimate living friend among the seven or eight of did-you-speak-to-them-again, and therefore the one whom I can least keep at arm's length, hardly indeed at wrist length. Perhaps, after all, this is not my apologia but an apology.

R. C. SHERRIFF

WHEN that sweet and lovely comedian Sid Field was playing in *Harvey* at the Prince of Wales Theatre, I went to see it (or went to see *him*) seven times, simply because I could not keep away, and because the management were indulgent over letting me have a couple of seats whenever the craving became too much for my sense of moderation in all things. Early in the long run of the play I made friends with Sid and would go round to his dressing-room during a long interval, where sometimes I found him alone and disposed to serious conversation, and sometimes affectionate and convivial with a rollicking assembly of friends. As I was always generously allotted two seats, I would try to find somebody who had never seen Sid; the same sort of game I played when I went over and over again to see the Lunts. And in both cases where I felt my guest deserved the honor and was as enthusiastic as even I could demand, I would send backstage and ask permission to bring round a friend.

So when I invited R. C. Sherriff to accompany me on one of these repeated expeditions (and he was delighted with Harvey, as I knew he would be) I scribbled a line to Sid telling him he would be seeing us presently, sure of a warm reception—Sid was the soul of courtesy—but with no idea of what it might mean to him.

Sid was alone in his dressing-room when we came in; he moved forward to welcome us, and at once something told me there was no need for me to introduce Bob formally, any more than one would have said to anyone: "Oh by the way, you two haven't met yet, have you? This is King George VI."

"Twenty years ago," said Sid Field in hushed and reverent tones, "I came three times to this very theater to see your *Journey's End*. I can't believe that you're here tonight just to see me."

(Ah, did you once see Shelley plain
    And did he stop and speak to you?)
For the rest of that interval, while the two men sat on the sofa earnestly engrossed in shop, I was content to sit a little apart, for it was good enough to watch Sid's face. I felt consciously instrumental, and certainly not in the least desolate and out of it. To suppose that I had created the moment would have been too Godlike an arrogance; I still imagined, however, that I had directed it; from any theological viewpoint, just as arrogant!

And yet this encounter was only to last about twenty minutes, and I wonder why I have always remembered it and set it among really important things? Perhaps because it illustrates my hero-worship motif.

My own first meeting with the author of *Journey's End* happened in 1929; while the London run of the play

was still going on, at a luncheon arranged by John van
Druten, himself a dramatist of repute whose *Young
Woodley* had been a sensational success the year before.
I cannot remember anything more eventful marking our
conversation than that we "made friends" and have been
friends ever since; though often between our meetings
have occurred those long spaces of time from which I always seem to suffer more than the opposite party. It was
delightfully easy to make friends with this thin, genial,
restless man; easy as falling off a log; about his personality
was a sort of eager—*chumminess* is the only word, mixed
in equal parts with diffidence, but like John Betjeman, a
diffidence informed with vitality. And yet, tabulating a
complaint, I swear that for nearly thirty years it has been
I who had to take the initiative every blessed time I wanted
to see him; because—and who would have thought it from
his manner?—R. C. Sherriff is a natural solitary; I don't
believe I have ever met him arm-in-arm with another man,
or our modern equivalent of arm-in-arm; nor by chance
caught a glimpse of him across a restaurant lunching with
a party of friends. Oh, of course he *has* friends, plenty of
good friends, probably with the same interests as himself
in rowing, cricket, the theater; nevertheless I maintain
against odds and on evidence from others, that he does
not miss us when we are not there; I can imagine his astonishment when he reads in these pages that we all regard
him as something of a mystery man.

The first time I discovered it, my curiosity was shared,
or even promoted, by Noel Coward; and enthralled, we
discussed this enigma for an hour or more. I was spending the week-end with Noel at Goldenhurst; he had recently laid out a croquet lawn and was full of his prowess

at the game, kindly offering to teach me that afternoon,
so that when Larry Olivier and Adrienne Allen and Edna
Best and various others motored down the next day—"and
Bob Sherriff's coming, by the way; he's never been here
before"—we could have a foursome or even an eightsome.
Luckily for my pride, I was not altogether a novice; in
my teens we had had a croquet lawn in our garden and
I had been something of a champion at the game, though
I had not played for twenty-five years. Secretly I hoped,
however, that my old skill would not have deserted me;
as swimming and skating are said always to come back
once you have known how to swim and skate. It had
not deserted me; we played eleven games, and in ten I
beat him hollow. No need with Noel (of all people) ever
to save him from the misery of feeling too humble; one
might state, in fact, that for him this was a salutary experience; unwontedly silent, he did not lack in generosity,
for when his mother appeared towards the end of the
afternoon and watched us for a while, and distressed on
behalf of her usually all-conquering son, tried to point out
to him in an audible whisper that I was cheating and had
no right to go through a hoop at that juncture, he replied:
"I don't know what you're talking about, Mother; she's
a first-class player and I'm honored that she should want to
play with me at all."

Beautiful summer weather for the party who motored
down to lunch the next day. Giving us only a brief while
to recover from the feast, Noel masterfully led us forth,
down the garden to the croquet lawn, disregarding (as
was his winsome way) sundry protests of not being any
good at it, spoil the game, rather not play, etc. Over their
heads he called to me: "Peter, you and I had better pick

up sides," and chose Bob Sherriff to start with, as according to his deprecating account of himself he knew less than any of them about croquet.

"Oh, I start? Righti-o! but you must tell me what I *do* . . . Yes, I see—I hold the thing by this end, do I?" (the thing was the mallet, and I may be exaggerating, but this is the impression we had of his total ignorance and his willingness to learn). "Yes, *I* see. Which is my ball? . . . Oh, the blue one. And I have to get it into a position from where I might have a chance of getting through that hoop next time it's my turn; I hope I *can*!"—with a laugh for his anticipated clumsiness.

And then from the starting-point by the stick, at a long distance from the first hoop and at an almost impossible angle, he swung his mallet, hit the blue ball, and went straight through.

"I *say*," said Bob, "I'm through, aren't I?"

A fluke, of course. Still, he had not hit the ball wildly; there was a certain directness and strength about the shot. . . .

"Oh, am I to hit it again, before anyone else plays? What do I do now?"

Noel indicated curtly that he was to get as near as he could to a good position in front of the second hoop. "You'll be hit away by the others, but never mind."

"That hoop right down there at the end of the lawn? O.K., here goes." Again he swung his mallet, and again the ball went straight through the narrow hoop.

Silence on the croquet lawn. Nobody moved. I dared not look at Noel, I might have laughed.

"I *say*!" exclaimed Bob, "that's good, isn't it!" Then suddenly a change came over him; he looked at his wrist-watch, and innocent gratification turned to apology: he was most awfully sorry, but he had to be off; he had no idea it was so late; a chap coming to see him at home . . . his mother wouldn't know what he wanted . . . it had taken longer to get here than he'd expected—"Look, I'm so sorry; it won't spoil your game, will it? Cheerio!"

That evening, when the rest had also departed, I asked Noel: "Do you think he knew?"

"Do *you*?"

"I'm not sure."

"*I* believe he did. One shot like that could have been a fluke; not two. And rushing off directly afterwards in case he couldn't pull off the hat-trick—!" Noel maintained that it was a piece of superb production on Bob's part; but I kept on changing my mind. I still don't know. Especially since that similar episode, not many years ago, when he gave a paper to the Royal Society of Literature, with Malcolm Muggeridge in the Chair. Of course I intended to be present, and directly the card came announcing it, rang up Bob to ask if he would care to come to tea here first, with Pamela Frankau, and we could all go together. Apparently surprised that I should care to attend at his obscure little activities, Bob replied that he would be *much* too nervous to be coherent beforehand, so he would rather not see me till after it was all over; and then added, bewildered: "I say, what *happens* at this place? They just wrote and asked me if I'd come and talk to them."

"Look here, Bob, you must be a Fellow or they wouldn't have."

"Oh yes," Bob agreed, as though to have been elected to that honorable and old-established body were something that might happen to anybody when they weren't looking, "I *am* a Fellow. But I don't know anything about it, I've never been near them" (he had heard of croquet, but never, of course, had a mallet in his hand!).

A packed audience. Bob sat on the platform looking diffident—(I apologize for using the word so often)—fidgetting and twisting his long legs about, while Malcolm Muggeridge introduced him in an excellent speech from the Chair. There was a burst of applause . . . and then that expectant hush which we all learn to dread as we rise to our feet and forget our opening sentences. It may have been more expectant and curious than usual, for whereas the Chairman was already well known for his gift as a speaker, none of the audience had ever yet heard as much as a squeak from this tall thin man, smiling at us shyly and obviously wishing it were all safely over. Taking us into his confidence as though we were two or three pals sitting round a tea-table, he remarked with his characteristic genial modesty that there didn't seem any reason, did there, why he should say any more at all, we had had such a good time listening to Mr. Muggeridge? . . . His preamble lasted for two or three minutes. I wasn't worried; this was the way he achieved *Journey's End*; this was the way he had examined his croquet mallet, asking for instruction by which end he should hold it . . . and then had gone through two hoops at an almost impossible angle from an almost impossible distance.

No orator in the accepted sense he did not "dominate" his audience; but completely natural and at ease, took them into his confidence and provoked shouts of laughter with every point he made. At first they were incredulous, then surrendered to this wizard's trick of presenting autobiography with such an engaging twist of humor and such disconcerting insight of what the other man was up to . . . By the time he had finished telling of his first adventures in Hollywood, Malcolm Muggeridge was thumping the table in his delight; and at the end, when he could make himself heard through the laughter and applause, offered Mr. R. C. Sherriff a post on the regular staff of *Punch* at any time when he would care to honor them by accepting it.

"I say," said Bob when we re-met, "was it O.K.?"

All very well, but Ll.-G. performing in the same idiom knew exactly what he was aiming at. Once again, did Sherriff? Opinions remain divided. And though the issue was wholly unimportant, it seemed vital to come to an understanding on the truth of the matter. Otherwise how can one ever be sure if *Journey's End* were not also achieved as it were by divine accident? So the investigation continues, with here and there a clue . . . And by the way, though according to immemorial habit one "gives a paper" for the R.S.L. and never speaks extempore, I learned that the manuscript which Sherriff had laid in front of him and consulted from time to time, was an old seed catalogue; the unsophisticated little fellow confessed his harmless expedient one afternoon when he arrived late for tea, flushed and exultant, his arms overflowing with bulging parcels. "I've been shopping for my mother," he explained, "and look here, I've got a present for you." Spilling parcels all over the hall, he fumbled in an inner pocket and produced a small, neat packet wrapped and sealed. "I suddenly thought, I've never given Peter a present!" His manner, ingenuous, triumphant, hardly able to wait until I got it open, reminded me irresistibly of a child proud of its handiwork—"Look, Mummy, it's for you!" so that I almost expected to see emerge from the wrappings a kettle-holder worked painfully in big stitches and showing traces of pricked fingers bravely endured for Mummy's sake . . . It was however not a kettleholder, but a costly little flagon of Floris' scent; and linked to the croquet episode and the sensational success of his Royal Society of Literature speech, I could not be sure whether this exhibition of naïve delight were not a further piece of corroborative evidence that he had probably spent a whole debonair lifetime carelessly presenting ladies with perfumery and diamond necklaces.

Yet there was nothing immature in his shrewd appraisal of his own sensational success—a "freak success" he called it himself when he mentioned *Journey's End* in the speech —and his interpretation of the Grandees who took him up and invited him to stay in Grandee country houses: "He's a funny little fellow, you know'," thus he improvised with startling clairvoyance their presumable descriptions. " 'Used to be a clerk or something like that; lives with his mother somewhere in Surrey, I think; bought a villa with what he made from that play, and they actually keep two servants and a car! Goodness knows where he went to school, but he's quite presentable in a way.' "

It was, I believe, at one of these house-parties that he first met Rudyard Kipling, who took him aside and talked to him and to no one else. Sherriff was not by nature a hero-worshipper, but of course the author of *Puck of Pook's Hill* had a special significance to a man whose passion was not for contemporary history but for chronicles of the Ancient Romans in Britain; so he was pleased when Kipling invited him to spend the week-end at Burwash, though an attack of quiet claustrophobia over staying with strangers led him to whittle it down to an afternoon visit.

"What was Kipling like?" I asked. I had been present

at his first meeting with Bob, but never met him again.

"Well, of course he wasn't a bit like a great man, they never are. I was sent up to him when I arrived; he was in the attic washing the dogs and talked to them a good bit, and to me in between whiles. And then, just like any other chap who was fond of the country, he took a great knobbly stick and marched me off for a long walk. And when we were still on his own land and passed a big tree, he'd hit the trunk in a friendly sort of way and say: 'Grand old fellow!' He was very proud of the width of his yew hedges and kept on—" I forget whether Bob said he kept on laying his stick across the top or poking it through the middle; anyhow, the object was to prove the yew hedge was the wider.

After the tremendous freak success of *Journey's End*, in the next few months he was introduced to so many celebrities, not in single file but a throng, so many names familiar in the mouth as household words, that his capacity for hero-worship, if it had ever existed, was diverted into a continual sequence of dazed recognition and then matter-of-fact acceptance; thus, on being presented to King George V: "Oh yes, that's the face on our half-crowns!" —a typical reaction from a potential numismatist.

Just one more memory of Sherriff's charmingly diffident voice and manner paying tribute to my superior learning. It came on the morning after one of the great events of his career, the First Night of the German production of *Journey's End* in Berlin in 1928. *Die Andere Seite*, they called it; subtle and clever of them: *The Other Side*. We had already seen the play in French, and presently it was to be translated into some thirty languages, Japanese and Braille included, and played in almost every capital in Europe with "crowned heads" (not

as sparse then as now) sitting in the Royal Box and summoning the dramatist to be presented to them; but played
in German, in what had been the enemy's capital, obviously one felt an increased tension. Queer to be sitting
there wondering how the audience would take it; and
indeed, how the players would act it? British officers,
British soldiers, making a last desperate stand in the
trenches with the Bosch only a few yards away; a German
prisoner captured and brought in for questioning by the
British Colonel; muttering German gunfire, louder at the
end when the roof of the dug-out collapsed on the dead
body of young Raleigh left alone when Stanhope made
his final sortie into certain death . . . The onlookers, silent
and attentive, received it coldly at first; especially were
they out of touch when Osborne, the older man, steadied
young Raleigh's excitement before a dangerous recon-
naissance by talking of otter-hunting and quoting Alice in
Wonderland—Ach, these English with their children's
stories! the German translation swapped Alice for the
Midsummer Night's Dream, as slightly more credible for
grown men. But they warmed into immense enthusiasm
at the dramatic scene between Stanhope and Hibbert, the
coward. And at the final curtain *Die Andere Seite* had a
terrific ovation.

Four of us were sharing a hotel suite for a few days;
and the next morning came a knock at our sitting-room
door, and Bob appeared with his I'm-sorry-am-I-disturb-
ing-you expression, and about thirty newspapers under
his arm: "I say, you know their lingo, don't you? I
wonder—would you mind looking through these and
telling me what they say? Or were you just going out?"

Professionally we never got this diffidence act from
him; professionally he knew his stuff from A to Z, almost

from the start of his career; and when he spoke with authority it was a treat to listen and marvel at the transformation; impressive because it did not depend on throwing his weight about, which of course is never impressive. He was quite rightly determined that the next Sherriff play which all the managers were vociferously demanding, shoud not be an echo and an anti-climax; so with *Badger's Green* he went out of his way to make it as different as possible; in its own genre it was equally good, with the same certainty of touch, this comedy of a cricket match in an English village; but as one might have expected, it was a total flop. *Not another Journey's End!* the newspaper captions informed the world the next morning. Bob took it philosophically; he had just moved into Rose Briars, a house with a large garden at Esher, and he and his mother comforted themselves, as they walked up and down the lawn and made plans, by saying that at least they had got this out of it, for a little while anyhow. He had lately resigned from his post as surveyor to an Insurance Company, partly because his desk was in the window and he used to be pointed out as "the chap who wrote *Journey's End*"; and decided he would fulfill an old dream: go to Oxford and read history. He had— has, in fact—a passion for history. Unfortunately, human nature being what it is, he was by now rather too old and rather too famous for the experiment; to his disappointment the undergraduates were respectful and called him Sir. And though he liked the boating and cricket and so forth, he was also disappointed in his own slow progress as a student of history. So he accepted an invitation from Hollywood to come out and make a film script of Remarque's *All Quiet on the Western Front*; and once there, took on a second assignment, H. G. Wells's *Invisible*

Man. After this somewhat unusual experience for an undergraduate, he returned to Oxford for a couple of years, and when he left, endowed an R. C. Sherriff Scholarship for literature.

The story of his second film script was related by Sherriff himself at the R.S.L. with his characteristic good humor which concealed a caustic criticism: how he was received by the Studio with great enthusiasm and handed about a dozen scripts which had already been made of *The Invisible Man* by a dozen different writers, but which somehow hadn't quite satisfied them: they asked him to read them through and then at his leisure and in his own time see what he could do about it. Sherriff did read them through, and was puzzled; the twelve treatments might have been made from twelve entirely different books: he could discover no resemblance between them. So he went and knocked round the second-hand bookshops in Los Angeles and succeeded in finding a battered old Nelson's Sevenpenny of *The Invisible Man.* "I took it back and read it, and then I copied it out. Of course I did a bit of cutting and padded it with a few camera directions to make it look like a shooting script before I handed it up. They went wild over it, sent for me and said 'But this is *marvellous!* Where did you get it?' And I said, 'From the book,' and they said, 'What book?' "

I don't believe the last line—although it got a big laugh; anyhow, it was near enough to the truth not to lay him open to a prosecution by the Society for the Prevention of Cruelty to Hollywood.

That was how he came to be a film ace. And here again you could never call him a distinguished amateur but always a professional, mysteriously knowing his job and speaking with complete authority; nevertheless I think he would rather have been an historian and dwelt in the semi-obscurity of the academic world; limelight is no treat to him; his hobbies are his treats—the Kingston Rowing Club, pulling his weight in the boat while he was still young enough, and later running along the tow-path in all weathers shouting directions; I gather the crews were always extremely respectful to their coach—"He knows his business," they said. Sherriff always *does* know his business.

Ever after, three strings to his bow: plays, films and novels; his first novel, *The Fortnight in September*, written after *Badger's Green*, was as nearly perfect as a novel could be; a completely unpretentious account of the Stevens family on their annual holiday at Bognor; Mr. and Mrs. Stevens and their children, Mary, Dick and young Ernie. It had no other plot apart from the author's uncanny sense of knowing exactly and in detail what each member of that family *enjoyed*, and how and in what circumstances they enjoyed it, mentally and physically, apart and together; knowing what can make holiday into holy day. We have seen already that his instinct was "in-fal-*li*able" (as J. M. Barrie's policeman said in *A Kiss for Cinderella*) over the hopes and fears, the ambitions and sudden exhilarations of boys and young men and older men—Osborne in *Journey's End*; in *The Fortnight in September* he gently invades the body, mind and soul of Mr. Stevens, the middle-aged father of the family. And in Mary, the daughter of nineteen, for once, I think, Sherriff clearly realized also the turmoil of a girl's mind; especially in the chapter where she makes friends with a bolder, handsomer wench, and forsaking the wonted pleasant evening stroll with her family, companions this "Billie" in search of "romantic" adventure, a pick-up along the darker parts of the promenade . . . The tension

and thrill in this particular seaside holiday game are as
vividly imagined by the author and set down with as
little apparent effort as he would have needed to describe
a cricket match for a boys' school magazine. Infal-*li*able
indeed! because his almost nonchalant certainty of touch
then takes us back to the timid, self-sacrificing mother of
the family, little Mrs. Stevens, left at her own request to
spend the evening resting at home after she has put Ernie
to bed; and shows what it means to her, quietness and slip-
pers and no chores, relaxing from busy evenings in her
own kitchen, and luxuriously sipping her delicious allowance of port, a special holiday prerogative; the writer's
own experience, sex, age and temperament so successfully
cleared out of the way for the vacant space to be entirely
possessed by Mary and then by her mother, that in spite
of all one's usual hesitations and apologies and clearing
the throat for daring to use such a word, I am afraid I
must call him a genius. And though *The Fortnight in September* appears to be autobiographical in place and incident, from the madly excited inspection by Ernie of the
back gardens seen from the train windows along the line
between Dulwich and Clapham Junction, down to the
last sad moment of yielding up the key of the Cuddy
(their beach hut) until next year, the characters themselves are not drawn from life; at any rate not the parents
—I have many times heard descriptions of Mr. Sherriff
senior from Mrs. Sherriff whenever I went down to stay
at their house in Esher, and she, the kindest, most comfortable hostess in the world, is so obviously a more confident, positive, warmer personality than little Mrs.
Stevens could ever have been. I always enjoyed staying
at Rose Briars and spending idle pleasant hours watching
Bob's expert ministrations to, it might be, a sick sycamore;

for a love of gardening, and especially tree gardening, has to be added to his overcrowded time-table. And while he was absorbed in his patient, I tried to lure his mother back into the past to tell stories of Our Hero's Boyhood. Here is my favorite, redounding neither to the discredit of Mrs. nor Mr. R. C. Sherriff, or I should have resisted— though not without difficulty—the temptation to repeat it during their lifetime. It arose from a question of punctuality; I think Bob had been late for lunch, and his mother told me that the tendency had started when he was a boy, because his father had been severely punctual and insisted that his family should conform and always be dead on time for meals: "So it set up a resistance complex," Mrs. Sherriff explained—Well, no; what she really said was: "Bob rather liked annoying his father, and used to be late on purpose." It was only the other day that in a relevant context I repeated to Bob what his mother had said, and asked him if it were true? After a moment's reflection: "No," a little injured, "it isn't true; I'm *extremely* punctual, but my father liked to be much too early for everything."

Thus history books get themselves made, differing so strongly according to which side they are on, and both versions sounding equally plausible. Yet somewhere lies a patch of darkness, and further evidence would only confuse us; we can never know, until Absolute Truth replaces our finite vision, whether Mr. Sherriff Senior or Mr. Sherriff Junior was always dead on time. The periods in history which appeal to Sherriff, he says, are always the long, slow twilights, the decay of greatness; the flushed, elated, jubilant eras have never interested him, with their victorious hordes, triumphant Emperors, too blatant to compete with the melancholy fascination of the gathering dusk before the night. When he wrote *Saint Helena*, in collaboration with Jeanne de Casalis, it was not Napoleon in the days of his glory, but Napoleon in exile who appealed to his sympathy; Napoleon pathetically boasting when after much effort he coaxed a weak lettuce from the soil of the Longwood garden. *Saint Helena* was the first modern play to be put on at the Old Vic under Lilian Baylis; and her faithful audiences were not used to it; for the first three nights it played to an almost empty theater. Then the Chancellor of the Exchequer wrote a letter, published in *The Times*, thundering his praise of this magnificent play and demanding that everyone should go and see it. As he happened at that time to be Winston Churchill, long queues formed at once at the Box Office and waited outside the doors for the Pit and Gallery. The house was packed and sold out, and this went on for six or seven weeks. But as the initial idea of the Old Vic was for Shakespearean and other classical repertory, and not for a Popular Success, *St. Helena* moved to a West End theater and that broke the spell.

To the theme of decline but not fall, when the tumult and the shouting dies, the captains and the kings depart, and you find out, so to speak, what history has been up to, Sherriff has been attracted over and over again. One of his most moving plays called *The Long Sunset* presents a little group whose ancestors had settled in Britain after the Roman Conquest, and gradually in the course of two or three centuries grew to look on it as their home, not realizing that the great Roman Empire had meanwhile broken up and the Legions were being recalled, abandoning the country to the invading Saxons. The end of the play, the baptism scene between Julian and his wife Serena, reminds me of the last scene and curtain in *Jour-*

ney's End, only not as hopeless; for to surmount the inevitability of death waiting for them at their last quiet picnic supper together, up in the woods on the Kentish Downs near the Roman port of Richborough, it has spontaneous prayer.

Serena: Will you listen, Master? We haven't got a priest, but we're in great trouble. My husband wants to go with you when we leave here. He wants you to let us go together.

Julian: Is it all right?

Serena: I think he would have told us in some way if it wasn't.

Julian: Does he refuse many people?

Serena: I don't think he's ever refused anybody who really wanted him.

Julian: Will you tell him it was only a bit of fun when I made jokes about him?

Serena: He'd understand that.

Julian: Then that's everything, is it?

Serena: I ought to baptise you.

Julian: That's a long business. That old priest was splashing about for hours.

Serena: It needn't take long. It's quite simple really. We've got some water here.

(*She goes across the room and fills a cup from a jar on the sideboard.*)

Julian: That came out of Sylvanus' spring. It wouldn't be any good, would it?

Serena: I don't think it matters where it comes from.

It will be seen that Sherriff refuses to conform to the traditional view of historical characters, wherefore King

Arthur in *The Long Sunset* comes as something of a
shock; neither Malory nor Tennyson would recognize
the portrait; and though I am ready to declare that we
can acquit the dramatist of defying legend without reason
or research, I do suspect in a description of Arthur's wife,
Guinevere, his wicked enjoyment at thus thumbing his
nose at Tennyson:

("Guinevere's a Christian, too . . . Arthur's wife. She
runs a school for the children. She's more educated than
Arthur. He doesn't bother much about anything but
the fighting, but Guinevere thinks a lot about what's
going to happen when the fighting's over. She wants
better people than the ones we've got today. So if *we*
had children, they'd be all right.")

Pass that. But I am spoiling for a fight over an equally
unorthodox whitewashing of King John:

The history books tell you that he was the worst King
we ever had, but he could hardly have been as bad as
he was painted. The only accounts of his personal character that have come down to us were written by
monks who hated him because he attacked and robbed
the monasteries. They naturally made the most of what
was bad about him and left out what was good, but
even if there wasn't a great deal of good about him any-
way, *it doesn't seem as if all his troubles were of his own
making* . . . He would call upon the Abbot or Prior, in
the King's name, to open the gates and give hospitality
to him and his hungry men. Having eaten and drunk
the place bare and dry he would confiscate everything
of value and go his way. If the monks were rash enough

to hide their treasure on news of his approach, then they had the choice of disgorging it without delay or seeing their monastery go up in flames.

—Surely, if King John attacked and robbed the monasteries because he was hard up, his troubles *were* of his own making? Like everybody else, he had the free will *not* to pillage and burn them but remain unable to pay his mercenaries to keep a throne which he had originally usurped from his elder brother Richard the Lion Heart, far away on the Crusades. According to R. C. Sherriff (and I mention this respectfully in obeisance to his expert knowledge) there were fifty wagons and eighty pack horses; some carried stores, but most of it was treasure—a vast hoard of treasure to have been carted round England simply as a matter of necessity to pay his men. Nor were the monasteries his only source of supply. There were also the Jews. *Good* King John (I have always been taught) used to pull out their teeth one by one till they let him have the gold he unlawfully claimed, only so that the agony should stop. It may be that my information has been too trustfully based on Little Arthur's History of England, Shakespeare's *King John* and Kipling's *The Treasure and the Law*; whence it does seem to emerge that my least favorite King of England was greedy, unscrupulous, treacherous, dishonest and cruel. Not very endearing qualities for a monarch! Pondering on these matters, I had just lashed myself into a fine state when John Betjeman came to lunch, and not for a moment suspecting two of them in collusion at this whitewashing business, I asked him:

"What do *you* think of King John?"

"Oh, I like him," replied Mr. Betjeman, his very voice a caress.

"*Like* him?" incredulous; "yes, but look here—"

"Directly they say 'a weak king' I start liking them. Edward II and Richard II were two of the finest kings we ever had in England, and William IV was the best of all." I had no objection to his preference for our sailor king, and allowed Betjeman to prattle on; at any rate he was on the right side (mine and Hugh Ross Williamson's) in the Richard III controversy which in recent years has become a prominent feature of the landscape. But then, returning to the Plantaganets: "I can't bear those warlike heroes, Richard I and Henry V. John was a nice man."

"He was a cruel man. It's not like you to defend cruelty. He tortured people for their wealth."

"So did Edward I and Edward III, as much as John; probably more."

"And does that make it right?" becoming more of a prig every moment, an indignant prig.

"Edward III was the worst king we ever had"—(I must have been misinformed all these years)—"They told me—"

"Who told you?"

"Historians," replied John Betjeman. "I read history at Oxford, you know."

"So did Bob Sherriff."

"Yes, we must meet; I like the sound of him."

"I'm sure you'd get on," bitterly, deprived of an ally, a couple of real historians against me, and a strong recommendation to consult various dons. Nothing silences me so wholly as the citation of academic authority; and for the moment I could hardly decide which of my two friends I hated most for debunking all my most glamorous kings and clapping little gilded wings on King John's shoulders . . . With ferocious pleasure I remembered how

he had been humiliated at Runnymede. And I still continue to object strongly to Sherriff's air of tolerant indulgence, which will undoubtedly amuse him, as he was
amused in retrospect by our only other disagreement; I
had forgotten all about it till I re-read the personal inscription on my copy of *King John's Treasure*:

> You are, I think, a good deal responsible for this book
> because when you said you didn't like my sentimental,
> sophisticated soul-shaking story of the officer and the
> chorus girl I said to myself all right then, I'll write an
> unsentimental, unsophisticated roast beef and two veg.
> book about a boy and another boy.
>
> It took a long time but here it is, and if you think
> that Peter and Simon are unpleasant boys then it's no
> good making a fuss about it because if it hadn't been
> for you they probably wouldn't have been born. So
> there. From your devoted Bob.

And I smiled, recognizing the usual reaction of Any
Author to Any Criticism of whichever of their books
has been a flop. Even if secretly we don't think much of
it ourselves, we are apt to retort icily: "It happens to be
the best thing I've ever written!"—("Little Bessie's the
only plain one of your eleven handsome children." "As it
happens," icily, "Little Bessie is by far the handsomest of
the lot.")

I was glad he had made me responsible for *King John's
Treasure*, because I find it an absorbing tale, and agree
with the blurb which said it had the double fascination
of a treasure hunt combined with a detective story.
Chiefly I enjoyed the first half, as Peter and Simon and
their history master were led by a blend of ancient

archives, excavations, archaeology, old wives' tales, legend
and luck, to locate the treasure supposed to have been lost
in the Lincolnshire marshes:

> "If I were to make a guess, I would say that gold and
> silver worth two or three million pounds is lying under
> those cornfields round Sutton Bridge. Most stories of
> buried treasure are fairy tales. This is the only one I
> know that's really true"

Following his natural bent for excavation and on a
measure of practical experience, the author dug his story
for *The Long Sunset* out of the buried ruins of a Roman
villa on the South Coast, and will tell you that he cares
for this play more than for any other he has written.
Some years before, he had been advised to consult Sir
Mortimer Wheeler as to how to get hold of a really good
site; much in the same way, he said, as one would be sent
to a house agent reputed to have some really desirable
residences on his books . . . A taste for this period of archaeology had started when he was a little boy and went
on bicycling tours with his father, and they stayed at a
farm in the neighborhood of Silchester where there were
a great many Roman remains, and caught sight of an old
saucer in which the farmer had dropped a lot of small,
worn-out coins turned up by the plough, stamped (if
he studied them closely) with the heads of Tiberius,
Claudius and Nero, which filled him with awe and excitement and incredulous wonder.

The company towards whom he naturally gravitated
did things in groups: cricket teams, stage and film com-
panies, the men who were engaged with him in thrilling
excavation adventure. Yet even here, when the dusk came

and the noisy sightseers had all departed, he would say to the others: "You go home, I'll stay here and dig for a bit."

And that for him was the supremely romantic hour, when the professional merged into the visionary, and he would feel that directly beneath his feet were villas and cities where Roman families had actually lived for hundreds of years . . . the ancient world rising from under the turf.

> They were men and women, they have gone their
> ways now
> As men and women must. The high song is over.

When it was dark, too dark for digging, he laid down his tools and contentedly walked back alone across the English fields.

SOMERSET MAUGHAM

N A PREFACE to the handsome uniform edition published to celebrate Somerset Maugham's eightieth birthday, he wrote:

> I had been struck by the notion that the veneration to which an author full of years and honors is exposed must be irksome to the little alert soul within him which is still alive to the adventures of his fancy. Many odd and disconcerting ideas must cross his mind, I thought, while he maintains the dignified exterior that his admirers demand of him.

And reading this, I remembered with amusement how on his sixtieth birthday, his staff at the Villa Mauresque arrived in a deputation to present him with a basket of azaleas stiffly arranged, accompanied by a lugubrious speech from the butler to the effect that Monsieur Mogghum was now sixty and naturally could not be expected to live for many years longer; would he accept this ex-

pression of their esteem and united good wishes? His
eighty-fourth birthday, on January 25th of this year, can
therefore be vulgarly described as nuts to the butler.
When he was seventy-seven, he wrote to me in thanks
for my congratulations, but complaining rather unreason-
ably that he did not care for the odd numbers: "I now aim
at eighty!"

His marksmanship appears to have been good.

When trying to paint a true portrait, it is somehow always the trivial irrelevant moments that first leap to the
mind; thus, ransacking memory for some illuminating
aspect in proper relation to the whole, up springs instead,
like a jack-in-the-box, an imaginary little picture I cher-
ish of our hero on that sixtieth birthday, standing outside
an antique shop in Nice, his nose pressed flat against the
window, sucking his thumb and wishing someone would
give him fifty centimes. That evening we all had dinner
at Monte Carlo, and, contrary to his usual custom, he
went into the *Salle Privée*, settled himself at a table where
chemin de fer was in progress, and sat there imperturbably
winning . . . till apparently he deemed he had exactly
enough for his secret purpose, gathered up his counters,
cashed them for the equivalent of about £40, and we
went home.

"What are you going to do with it?" I asked; "I often
wonder what the vintner buys—?" Then he told me that
he had long coveted a pair of beautifully carved dolphins
which he had seen through the window of an antique shop
in Nice, and which would look perfect in the inner courtyard at the Villa; but they cost the equivalent of £40.
Now, *now* he could afford to buy them . . . his melancholy
dark eyes sparkled and his voice rang out triumphantly;
nor, for once, could he understand my amusement; for

he always practiced a fairly severe discipline on matters of self-indulgence—(his autobiography has explained why) though spending on others he could often be surprisingly reckless. I remember when he came back to the Villa from a visit to India, he bade me go upstairs and choose a scarf from a lavish display spread out as gifts for his friends. And: "*That* one, Peter?" when I came down with a scarf so subtle in color and design that he might easily have worn it himself "you *do* surprise me!" He hesitated how best to round off the insult: "I was quite sure you would have chosen the gaudiest."

My tender flesh is stippled with these friendly little darts, especially when our correspondence happened to turn on literary subjects; that time, for instance, when I unfortunately mixed up Lord Orford with Lord Oxford; and a letter came back from Mr. Maugham headed "More in Sorrow than in Anger"; could it be possible, he wrote, that I had not recognized the reference to Horace Walpole? He thought that every schoolgirl knew who Lord Orford was.

I possess also a brilliant pastiche beginning: "My dear Charlotte" and signed "Your obedient servant William Makepeace Thackeray." And after I had sent him yet another of my numerous books about Robert Louis Stevenson, I chuckled at his aptness in beginning a letter of thanks: "My dear Mr. Dick," and ending it "From your loving little David."

But I had to control myself not to kick back when I mentioned that in his book of essays, *The Vagrant Mood*, there was only one I could not read; the rest I had found fascinating. "The one on Kant, I expect?" "No, I liked Kant; the one on Burke." "You *surprise* me, Gladys," blandly incredulous over my sad ignorance, as he had been over my choice of a scarf—("Gladys" instead of my nickname "Peter" always presages a bit of trouble on the way); "that essay on Burke was acknowledged by everybody who knows anything about it as by far the best in the book."

Yet he teases with a touch so light and clever as to be charming, with flashes of youthful impudence; affectionately trusting to his opposite number for the same light skill and an equal enjoyment—"Pastime with good company I love and shall until I die" . . . Nevertheless, there does exist an almost legendary Place of Awful Politeness, interesting, no doubt, but hardly salubrious; one may blunder in at very rare intervals and be thankful to stumble forth again, more by luck than by judgment, into the genial air.

Occasionally it was I who scored. Somerset Maugham has been known as a great traveler in the more or less unfrequented quarters of the globe; all the same, he completely lacks a bump of locality; I once gave him a compass to help him find his way through the trackless jungle, but doubted, with his peculiar disability, if it would even bring him safely from Drury Lane Theatre to the Savoy Restaurant! This hiatus in the Make-up of a Traveler was first revealed to me one fine morning on Cap Ferrat; he suggested that he and I might walk to Lennox Berkeley's villa for lunch, instead of driving over with the rest of our party; it would only take us ten minutes, he said. At the end of an hour it seemed to me that our stroll had become a little plodding and laborious, and he owned that he had not the remotest notion where we were, and hoped politely I was not getting tired—in those shoes? (My shoes were perfectly adequate; they were *espadrilles*, like his own.)

"If I'm right," he began presently, "the sea should be just round that bend on our left."

The sea was indeed just round that bend. On our right.

Yet these flippant manifestations of an outstanding personality might have been picked up by anyone, expressing as they do what Aristotle called merely the accidents not the substance of the man; not what makes Somerset Maugham just this Somerset Maugham and no other. As to that, he reserves the right to keep himself to himself—a particularly apposite cliché, for never have I read an autobiography which contains so little auto as his *Summing Up*. Though relishing the intimate autobiographies of his friends, he either cannot or will not supply them with a mutual satisfaction; years ago, Beverley Nichols gave a party to celebrate the publication of his own book of revelations, *Twenty-five*, and Willie Maugham's voice was heard above the merry din, announcing that Noel Coward was about to write the story of *his* life, calling it "Twenty-four."

An idiosyncrasy which a writer often does not realize till pointed out to him, is how one particular motif apparently lodged in his system, repeats itself over and over again in different guise, a gate-crasher that refuses to be snubbed, an unconscious traitor to his desire for reticence. Thus it may be noticed how often in his novels Somerset Maugham ardently refers to the power and religion of beauty:

It meant to him (Stroeve) what God means to the believer, and when he saw it he was afraid.

It seemed to her (Kitty) as though her body were a shell that lay at her feet and she pure spirit. Here was

Beauty. She took it as the believer takes in his mouth the wafer which is God.

And furthermore, he nearly always makes his articulate characters, immoral or amoral, eager to appreciate and comment on any outstandingly good character in the book; Dr. Saunders (*The Narrow Corner*) perceives not alone the pure and startling quality of Erik's goodness, but also that Fred Blake was struck all of a heap by it:

> ... the shock of admiration the lad had received when he was confronted with the realization of something quite startling ... You might have thought Erik a trifle absurd ... but there was no doubt about it, he had, heaven only knew by what accident of nature, a real and simple goodness. It was specific. It was absolute. ...

And in *The Painted Veil*, Kitty, a cheap little voluptuary, suffers a change of heart when she compares her frivolous third-rate social ambitions with the simple, impressive selflessness of the nuns nursing the plague at Mei-tan-fu. As for her husband:

> she thought suddenly of an instrument she had been shown in Hong-Kong upon which a needle oscillated a little and she had been told that this represented an earthquake a thousand miles away in which perhaps a thousand persons had lost their lives.

I should choose this inscrutable Walter Fane as the most intensely interesting of all Somerset Maugham's male characters; perhaps one might go as far as to say the most heroic, his quality unmarred by tiresome self-pity; the poignant irony that he and not his wife should die of the plague leads up to one of the great death-scenes in fiction, based on the text of "Let him who thinketh he stand-eth. . . ."

And here is yet another of Mr. Maugham's repetitive themes: Kitty in *The Painted Veil*, Strickland in *The Moon and Sixpence*, Rosie, the heroine of *Cakes and Ale*, each seeks a catharsis by plunging just once again into in-dulgence of the flesh after they have imagined they had nobly renounced it . . . then they emerge released, cre-ative, cured of sorrow. Rosie is indubitably his most at-tractive woman; he admits it himself; a warm-hearted, generous, irresistibly human creature, nobody would deny her the first place in his gallery of engaging rogues. Julia Lambert, too, undoubtedly goes into the Rogues' Gallery; and with the author of *Theatre* we can laugh at her swift and resourceful devices to extricate herself from trouble, and share his refusal to be pompous about her foibles: "I can only consider her, whatever she does, with fond indulgence."

Somerset Maugham is essentially business-like, an au-thor serious in the French sense (I was once warned in France not to go to a certain *horlogier* because he was not a "serious" watchmaker). For he has French blood in him; at moments one can actually *see* him being French when he advances across the room to meet a guest, his arms outstretched in welcome, a gesture difficult for an out-and-out Englishman without seeming self-conscious. A first-class craftsman, never for a moment does he treat authorship as a picturesque auxiliary to everyday life; the desk at which he concentrates on his work is permanently placed so that he faces the wall, his back to one of the loveliest views imaginable. He planned to stop writing plays when he was sixty, short stories when he was sixty-five, and novels after the half-dozen he had in mind were finished—I am not quite sure of the exact age at which each form of production was definitely to be given up, but I do know that apart from only five more novels instead of six, he adhered rigidly to his time-table, already fully aware of the enjoyment in store from his present dalliance with *belles lettres*; to some, such dalliance might have resulted in boredom, but in this case it has led to our delight and his. Which is just as well, for he has no philosophy to help him endure boredom.

By a reverse process, he has an equal capacity for entertaining or being entertained, according to his mood; I think that in medieval times he might have kept a jester, carefully selecting a high-class candidate from the Short List (what the interviews would have been like!) and not grudging a penny of the salary.

Visitors to the Villa Mauresque, however brilliant and famous, have to learn to respect his routine: he wrote during the whole morning, appeared in time for cocktails before lunch, a mellow, affable host, and retired for a couple of hours of recuperative sleep after lunch. Once, arriving about 11 a.m. at a hotel in Copenhagen and informed that our rooms could not possibly be ready until after six that evening, three of our quartet wandered about until sunset, restless and desolate from having no anchorage except the public rooms; but the fourth, who was Mr. Somerset Maugham, tranquilly extended himself for a post-prandial nap on a couch (made of boards) in the lounge, and in the midst of the usual hurly-burly of a busy hotel, slept from two to four o'clock, and woke fresh as a daisy.

That was the holiday when we traveled all over Scan-

dinavia with his notorious Book-bag, a sturdy affair of
canvas and leather, looking like a postman's sack; one
of his finest short stories is called "The Book-bag," pref-
aced with a description of how during a long convalescence following his dangerous illness in some far-off
corner of the East, he had found himself *with nothing to
read*, absolutely nothing except what was kindly fetched
for him from about a hundred miles away: a school edition, annotated, of all Racine's plays. Since then, he invariably travels with a Book-bag.

Life at the Mauresque is the essence of comfort without being casual or Bohemian; perhaps again it is the
French blood in our host which emanates a certain seem-
liness, a wish to have everything well balanced in time
and space; an *adult* household. He is completely adult,
too, in his literary preferences; it may be noticed that he
will not stand for children dashing up and down the pages
of his books, interrupting their elders; in this he resembles
Jane Austen, one of the few English writers for whom he
has the greatest admiration; and not only in this; geo-
graphically he may have roamed farther afield than she,
but they are affinities over commonsense, a preference for
civilized living, and a nice salty taste in wit and irony. In
his light reading, moreover, Mr. Somerset Maugham has
absolutely no use for whimsy, even of the high quality
from which *The Wind in The Willows* was shaped; to
him there is something faintly foolish in hankering for
children's books. It is one of my unworthy ambitions to
take him to see *Peter Pan* before I die.

When he returned from the South of France in September, 1940, on a cattle-boat which took three weeks for
the journey, he appeared in a new role, a blend of
Scheherezade and Listen-With-Mother; for at any time of

the day or night he could be relied on to gather his fellow passengers round him and keep them happy and interested and forgetful of submarines, while he told them stories. As revealed in *Ashenden*, a fictional version of his experience as British Agent in the 1914-1918 war, he is conspicuously cool, nonchalant and resourceful in danger, with the courage of endurance rather than of the type that would recklessly gallop in the Charge of the Light Brigade . . . when I believe that after duly pondering on the unwisdom of the order given, he would have deemed it the lesser folly to reason why.

And yet, a startling trait in one reputed (not without provocation) to be a cynic to end all cynics, he will at moments suddenly display a sky-blue patch of simple sentiment, and credulity and show himself capable of believing six impossible things before breakfast.

His contempt for colleagues who are victims of their own vanity has, I think, led him to under-estimate the place he deserves in modern English literature, as far as it can be estimated by ruler and compasses; soberly acknowledging his own merits and disabilities, he cannot in the very nature of things allow for the indefinable distinction which is bound gradually to emerge from the quantity of his output, as well as the quality. With a rare talent, pragmatic in origin, of being able to ask for useful criticism, no matter from whom provided he has judged it to be competent, he will accept any valuable part of the verdict and throw away the rubbish, but never take offense. It was during the very early days of our friendship, while I was still thrilled (and a bit shaky) at the honor of being admitted by him to anything like mental equality—("still" of course not meant in any disparaging sense; merely that one grows older)—that he sent me, unsolicited, a large package containing the complete typescript of his new book, *Don Fernando*. I could not have been more enchanted—until I read an accompanying *Questionnaire* in his own writing, asking for my advice on about thirty different points: Should he cut this? Should he leave out this? Was his meaning sufficiently clear there? Was such-and-such a chapter too long? I struggled through the four or five pages of closely written foolscap with a lively wish that I had died before I came to the Riviera for a holiday. . . .

At the end, my literary idol had neatly printed a demure R.I.P.

Fat lot of rest-in-peace I was to have during the next nightmare week! Luckily I became too engrossed in the impersonal job of answering his questions, to keep on remembering who had set the examination paper. And by his reception of my replies when I handed them in, I was once and for all impressed by the fact that no delicate flattery had been intended plus a secret determination to take little notice of whatever I might say; he was simply being professional. Captain Nichols, in *The Narrow Corner*, who goes well beyond the engaging stage of roguery, and fictionally speaking, is all a wonder and a wild delight (he cheats, he lies, he thieves, he murders, he is complacent and vindictive, he does not even know when he is disgusting and altogether horrible) yet shows one redeeming quality, from which we can gauge Mr. Maugham's respect for a man who knows his job:

> He seemed to take pleasure in his mastery of the little boat he managed with such confident skill; it was in his hands like a horse in a horseman's when he knows every trick and habit it has.

Maugham's taste for sober facts soberly phrased alternates with the robust, indeed, the Rabelaisian humor by which he views his characters and reports their speeches. For nearly always he must have a reporter present in his stories, a compère, a spectator, whatever you please. This sophisticated dispassionate narrator is, more often than not, himself; though he allows Dr. Saunders to deputize for him in *The Narrow Corner*. *Of Human Bondage*, being largely autobiographical, paradoxically does not require the presence of the first person singular; but in *The Razor's Edge*, as in *Cakes and Ale* and *The Moon and Sixpence*—"I boldly used my own name and made myself one of the characters that take part in the action."

The Moon and Sixpence, that bean-feast of cynicism, I like least of his novels; not, I hope, because I am too squeamish to swallow its brutal realism, nor wish the artist sentimentalized; but because I prefer Gauguin's legacy of glorious pictures without having to contemplate the mangled bodies of human sacrifice still smoking in front of them. And yet why, in the name of St. Carp and St. Cavil, should it be his only book provoking my strong desire to review it as though it were published yesterday? The answer may well be that one feels a certain diffidence in pouring out nothing but libations to a master teller-of-tales whose palate so distinctly prefers salt and mustard to an abundance of honeymead.

He will make no pact with cruelty; that is an article of his creed. Here is one story to stand for many when Don Somerset Maugham had the impulse to set forth in Quixotic rescue of a Dulcinea neglected because of no importance at a party that consisted entirely of celebrities; she was invited by her employer out of good nature, and then forgotten. With relief and a sense of warm com-

panionship she noticed that opposite her at the dinner-
table was another obvious non-celebrity, a quiet dark man
who appeared to have little to say to either of his neighbors; probably, like herself, he was overawed by the glit-
tering phalanx. After dinner when the ladies retired to
the drawing-room, her isolation became even more
marked; she sat alone, shy and unhappy, on a corner of
the sofa, while the rest chattered of their social diary.
Hours afterwards, or so it seemed, the men came in, her
co-mate and brother in exile caught sight of her and immediately crossed the room and sat down beside her . . .
They started talking about plays and playwrights; and
encouraged by his admirable attention, she grew animated
and held forth on her pet subject, laying down the law
on what was wrong with contemporary drama.

They left at the same time, and she asked if she could
drop him anywhere? "That's very kind of you," and he
got in beside her: while driving, she continued her discourse, feeling more eloquent and experienced every moment. Finally—"Do give me your name and I'll tell my
Club to send you an invitation to our next performance."
A short hesitation, and then: "I'm Willie Somerset
Maugham" . . .

(And did he stop and speak to you,
And did you speak to him again?)

"Oh *God*!" she exclaimed, aghast at the way she had
botched this first personal encounter with the great dramatist who had so long been her hero, "and I've spent the
whole evening telling you how to write plays!" But he
replied: "It was most interesting; I enjoyed it very much
indeed; thank you," and his tone satisfied her that the

pleasure had been genuine. It must be admitted however that several of us who are hero-worshippers by nature, have shown ourselves strangely inadequate to deal with these longed-for encounters when they did at last happen. [For myself with Max Beerbohm, John van Druten with Aldous Huxley, and now Dulcinea with Somerset Maugham, gremlins must have been invisibly officiating.]

I was a witness to another incident of the Cervantesque motive in W.S.M.: my secretary ("Tiger") and I were staying at a hotel near Villa Mauresque, and also near the villa of a not quite so famous author who was perhaps at that time a little too young to be kind, and rather inclined to slight Tiger. She and Somerset Maugham, however, were excellent friends; and because she was nearly a champion golfer, he behaved to her with all the pretty diffidence which was her due when they played together. One day he said to her: "You must go round with Martin some time"—(call him Martin!)—"Of course you'll beat him, but he can give you more of a game than I." "I don't want to," said Tiger . . . her inflection showing clearly enough for her companion's keen perception that she had been hurt. After a pause, he remarked gently: "He hasn't very good manners, has he, Tiger?" His tone drawing her into the circle of his real intimates who *had* good manners, and shutting Martin well outside. A beautiful piece of manipulative surgery.

Yes, cruelty born of snobbery will always get his goat . . . an exceptional animal, equal to any occasion; perhaps one day Graham Sutherland will paint it for us, going into action.

MONSIGNOR
RONALD KNOX

MANY years ago I was discussing with Father M. a fairly obscure point of Catholic scholarship, and rather out of my depth, asked him what Ronald Knox had had to say on the subject. "Ah well," he replied, "Ronnie Knox is of course hors concours."

And something slipshod in my mental French translation left me surprised at hearing Monsignor Knox spoken of as hors de combat! Later, amused at my mistake—which left Monsignor wounded on the field of theological argument, instead of placing him far above it—I told Knox himself of my error. And, "I expect I *will* be hors de combat next Wednesday," he remarked; "I'm flying for the first time, out to Uganda."

And I have since wondered what his mind did with that description of himself as hors concours, for it was certainly by no visible act of diffidence that his comment had left it discarded on the floor? I was still to learn that this great prelate of modern times, this famous wit and scholar, was celled with humility like honey in the comb; an innate humility; he could no more keep it concealed than some people can conceal their innate arrogance. Yet by some spiritual poise he was likewise immune from having to supply those tiresome protestations of inferiority which Freud forgot to remove sharply into a wholly separate classification; true humility exists in its own air of freedom, and when we are in its presence we remark perhaps "there must be humility in the room" as we might say "there must be violets in the room" . . . But an inferiority complex is a miserable sandwich-man with boards front and back; and if their announcements are blatant, the person has an extrovert inferiority-complex; but if the sandwich boards get lugged about with their message turned inwards so that we cannot see what it is, they have an introvert inferiority-complex, just as tiresome. Nobody ever heard Ronald Knox clamor for attention by falsely asserting that he could not excel where he manifestly could and had; that would be taking up time, and he was always loth to squander time on himself. Is it my fancy, or did Max Beerbohm contemplate starting a series of caricatures on *Unlikely Performances* with one entitled "Ronnie Knox Blowing His Own Trumpet"?

I first heard Monsignor Knox, in 1948 at a church in Kensington delivering a sermon on the Love of God; and because I had only recently become a Catholic and knew little about him, my young godmother and I had decided to go on a mere we-might-as-well; the theme implicit in the title was promising if this man could preach at all. Just as we were starting out in plenty of time to get a good front seat, a letter arrived which threw me into a paroxysm of rage; a letter from somebody who had the professional right to pass a verdict on the book which I knew was the

best I had ever written or ever likely to write; in his opinion, however, no masterpiece but rather boring. In a fury,
therefore, I sat down to pour out an answer, page after
page. Then, still breathing brimstone, I set out late to
hear this sermon by an unknown priest on the Love of
God . . . and what with wrath and having to sit crowded
in a pew right at the back of the church, nobody could
call it an ideal frame of mind for the message to sink in
and find a welcome and a home! Nevertheless and to my
amazement it did, and when I came back I tore up the
unposted letter.

Six years afterwards, and already personally acquainted
with Monsignor Knox, I wrote to him after my first Retreat at the Hampstead Cenacle and told him of this incident, because to my delight one of his Meditations had
been on the Love of God, and this time I was able to as-
similate the whole of it. Again however his humility
slanted off the point: he wrote back genuinely upset,
genuinely contrite that I should have been let in for
listening to an old talk and not given an entirely new one.

I'm afraid you had bad luck over that meditation on
the love of God. It *was* the same you had heard six
years ago (and others, I fancy, may have heard ten
years earlier.) It was so yellow and wrinkled into age
that I've just written a new one instead—but unfortunately I wrote it for the *next* retreat, not for yours.
However, you will get the new one if you are in retreat under me any time in this decade.

Difficult not to be disrespectful and cry out on reading
this: "Oh, don't be an *ass!*" As if one would care if one
had heard it twenty times already, or if he started a Re-

treat on the actual announcement: "*All* these talks are going to be old!" As if one would care! Could it be possible that he did not realize how in literary style and delivery and substance, he was—well, hors concours? Yes, it *was* possible; indeed he did not know and would not have believed it. . . .

Strange that "meek" of all works should be one where he failed to give us an inspired translation into modern English. It was in the sacristy of the little church to St. Thérèse de Lisieux, an altar in a Sussex field built by Sheila Kaye-Smith and her husband, Penrose Fry, that after Mass we were discussing with a Belgian priest an otherwise excellent sermon on the text: "Blessed are the meek," Father N. had kept on and on repeating "meek" and "meekness," and failed to understand, perhaps because English was not his own language, what I could possibly object to in the word?

"What is then so wrong with meek?" he asked.

"The meaning has deteriorated," I replied; and attempted to explain by metaphor: "It has had its hair parted in the middle and brushed smoothly down on either side!"

Oddly, this was of no assistance to Father N. "Humble," suggested Penrose as an alternative to meek; and even more unhelpfully, Sheila broke in "Oh no, *humble* is too Heepish!"

"*Heepish?*" repeated poor Father N., still pleading in vain for a little sensible elucidation.

So I asked, "How does Ronald Knox translate it?"

"Well, you know, Monsignor Knox is often very vulgar!"

Not unnaturally we yelped in protest: "What, *him?* Ronnie Knox *vulgar?*"

It took us a little while to realize that Father N. was thinking in Latin: vulgar, *vulgaris* (*vulgus*, common people). And indeed, Ronald Knox often used the language of common people like ourselves.

There may be, however, no exact rendering of "meek" into modern English; our vulgar Monsignor Knox had translated it as "patient"; and patient, I suppose, can be justified where impatience might argue a sort of arrogance, a lack of that humility which will always consent to wait its turn; taking Heep for ever out of humble and putting back what Dickens had withdrawn from it. When you are Ronald Knox, you can be both humble and debonair; *de bon air*, a startling translation of meek, occurs in a French translation published in Geneva about 1775, and sounds surprisingly right in spite of its present-day significance.

His manner was shy but debonair at our first personal encounter, when heaven knows by what small miracle he had consented at the intercession of a mutual friend to come to my home for lunch. Just before he left, I brought him my two most beloved bedside books for his autograph: *The Mass in Slow Motion* and *The Creed in Slow Motion*. And as he complied I could see what was his inward reaction: "My dear woman, you're doing this to please me and it doesn't; but never mind"—too courteous to show I was not thereby giving him pleasure; nor did it strike him that "R. A. Knox" in his handwriting on the flyleaf would add immeasurably to the value . . . and not the financial value, either! In a flash it then came to me that his essential humility was only not comical because its origin was so completely reasonable: unlike most of us, he possessed a constant basis for measurement, a clearer vision of what ultimately we were meant to be like; hence his steady accompaniment of *non sum dignus*. And a sentence he wrote in his Preface to *God's Threshold* (a volume of parables, symbolic stories, and fairytales) seems to bear this out: "We are only children, all of us hoping to grow up one day into the stature of the perfect man in Jesus Christ."

He had a talent which amounted to genius for lapsing almost absent-mindedly into a colloquial style, not only in his books but in his correspondence. I like to re-read an early letter in his scholastic restrained handwriting, starting off with a formal "My dear Miss Stern," and going on: "All right, have it your own silly way!"—an unwilling surrender in our serialized dispute on whether one of my rag-bag autobiographies touching on many themes, should or should not have been indexed? Ronald Knox maintained that it should; I argued that where one had meant to give an appearance of spontaneity in this sort of writing, an index would at once destroy the illusion. He continued to disagree—and then yielded: "All right, have it your own silly way!"—still complaining how he had especially wanted to comment on a certain passage somewhere in the middle of the book, and was baffled for want of an index:

> There's *Green Grow the Rushes oh*, for example, on which I'm a leading authority, but I can't find it again. . . . Did you know that there is a variant on No. 8 which reads "Eight for the gable rangers," and a fresh variant of this (presumably), which leads up to today's feast "Eight for the Angel Gabers"? A fact.

Far too rarely he gave a Retreat. They meant an outpouring of riches: four Meditations a day; and about twice I mooched in to see him between whiles with an air of I-couldn't-care-less, so that he did actually remark to the nun in charge when she made an appointment for me: "Oh, so she's not going to cut me dead this time? I was beginning to think she was!" But my pretended attitude was simply to reassure him that I did not intend to consult him deferentially and nervously as to the state of those knobs on my soul—though they could have done with treatment!—for he was never very robust, and Retreats were a drain on his nervous energy; so it was a relief, he said, to relax and talk human, and in his characteristic vein, impenitent and michievous, rag and be ragged and give as good as he got.

I saw him only seldom, and still want to sue British Railways for depriving me of a certain glorious opportunity when Heaven had provided two and a half hours secure from interruption, with the man whom I would certainly have chosen for such desert-island companionship. For en route to stay with a friend near Frome in Somerset, suddenly Monsignor Knox came along the corridor, and I like to think that his expressions of pleasure at seeing me were not just wishful thinking. He sat down opposite me, no other traveller was attracted by that particular railway carriage before we started non-stop to Frome . . . and then the wheels began to make more noise than any wheels of any train I have ever known; we shouted louder and louder, trying to make our voices rise above the din; said "What?" more and more frequently; but at last, noticing his expression of agreeable anticipation was gradually succeeded by strained politeness, I suggested that if he had a nice book handy, so had I, and we might as well complete the journey in silence. He admitted that he should be saying his Office, and that was that.

Frome was within driving distance of Mells; and in his first letter of invitation to come to lunch, he added:

"Unless you're staying west of Frome it's rather a long drive, but the place is well worth seeing." So to appease his humility, I made up a lot of nonsense about having other friends to visit west of Frome, so it would be quite worth my while coming to see the *place!* On a later occasion I remarked that I had seen Downside on the signposts, and so when the car fetched me after lunch I would like to drive over before going home, and pay my respects to the burial-place of Baron von Hügel. Apparently Downside was not more than a few miles away, but—score to me!—Monsignor Knox was not aware that von Hügel was buried there: "If you don't find him in the Abbey, try the cemetery attached to the Catholic church in the village a little way off," he suggested.

Whereupon I asked tentatively: "Couldn't you leave your work for a little while and drive over with me, just to show me where to look? I'm so bad at finding my way round."

"Well . . . I think perhaps I might," and his face lit up with that eagerness familiar to most authors when tempted to leave their writing if they can persuade themselves that the request provides a legitimate excuse.

Baron von Hügel and his family had presented a magnificent jeweled monstrance to Downside, and as a matter of course I imagined their tomb would be a noble pile with an elaborately carved description setting forth his less genial virtues. So when Monsignor Knox and I entered the Abbey, shadowy and beautiful, empty even of a zealous sacristan, almost at once we separated and went hunting along the aisles, pausing at every marble monument to scrutinize the inscriptions, mostly in praise of eminent prelates. At last: "No, he's not here," called out Monsignor, coming, so to speak, to the last tomb, "so we'll probably find him in the cemetery". . . . . And again I visualized a von Hügel catafalque grandly apart and railed off.

"Do you like the name Benedict?" my companion asked, as side by side again, we strolled towards the west entrance. "We've chosen it for Julian Oxford's baby."

I considered Benedict, and said yes, I did like it as a name, not as much as Nicholas or Dominic, but far far better than Gregory in the same group; I couldn't *bear* Gregory.

At which Ronald Knox pulled up, oddly excited by my vehemence: "Is it because of the two hard G's coming close together like that?"

"No," I replied, finding it easier to feel at home with him in a great Abbey than I would have thought possible with such a renowned dignitary of the Church, or with anyone who might have considered it more fitting and reverent to hush the voice to an unnatural whisper and creep about on tiptoe. "It's because I was given Gregory Powders when I was a child!"

"*So was I!*" Ronnie exclaimed, betrayed by the coincidence into a very passion of period fellowship; "so was I. Wasn't it beastly stuff and didn't it smell foul? I believe they forced us to take it on purpose to make us sick!"

Gregory Powders lasted us as far as the Catholic church in the village, where Monsignor sprang from the car and inquired of the parish priest who happened to be standing in the porch, if Baron von Hügel were buried there?

"Yes, he is; but you'd better let me come with you because you might find it difficult to pick out the tombstone; I often can't myself."

This puzzled me till I saw the little graves jostling one another, a hundred or more, most of them with just a plain cross of wood or stone at the head of a narrow mound, and hardly any room between for the grass and daisies. The sun beat down on us and it was very hot; we followed the priest . . . till at last he paused at one of these all but anonymous graves and bent down to read a name.

"Here you are; this is the one." And we too bent to see if it could really be the tomb of the illustrious Friedrich von Hügel. . . .

"Rather impressive, wasn't it?" Ronald Knox remarked quietly, as we drove away.

I agreed with his unspoken tribute, that no splendid edifice could have testified more impressively to the author of *The Mystical Element in Religion* than this plot of earth indistinguishable from all the others surrounding it. How . . . *gaudy* I had been in my expectations!

A small Catholic chapel was attached to the Manor House at Mells, and I remember how after Mass for the Feast of St. Peter and St. Paul, I was hospitably bidden to breakfast and how Monsignor looked up from the *Times* at my emphatic "Oh no, coffee *please*" on my hostess asking if I would prefer tea? "People who drink tea for breakfast instead of coffee should be segregated!" came forth as though he were pronouncing excommunication; a line that since then I have been prone to repeat in the wrong company, not realizing until I saw the hurt expressions of two or three present and watched them apologetically gulp and try to conceal their tea cups, that it would have been kinder left unquoted.

After breakfast on that particular June 29th, my friend's car arrived to fetch me away; and Monsignor

Knox came out to see us off. Standing at the door in the blazing sunlight, he noticed her little dachs on the seat of the car just below him, and put out an affectionate hand to pat his head; the dachs lifted a yard-long adoring nose towards him, and somehow to an onlooker the tableau was of a blessing spontaneously bestowed on the little creature. "There, Bill," we said after we had driven away (Bill's full name in the Kennel-book was Sigismund von Rakonitz, one of my Austrian ancestors), "now you must be an angelic hound all day, and not let down your side!"

The Vicar of Mells, in a moving and intimate valedictory to his old friend and neighbor, recalls how Ronald Knox had informed him that the Manor dog, a somewhat ponderous animal, grew strangely excited if one imitated a cuckoo . . . which he proceeded to show by experiment, only leaving off when it was clear that it might result in considerable damage to furniture.

He was greatly interested in Mells Church and its doings. When our churchyard wall was in danger, he urged the support of his friends, telling them solemnly that he did not want cows jumping over his grave. And more recently he enlisted the support of John Betjeman at a fête for the church clock and chimes, coming out, though gravely ill, for the opening ceremony in the rain.

We never discussed religious differences, each recognizing in the other that settled affection for the Church of our allegiance, which makes argument irrelevant and rather tiresome. It was part of his greatness of character that, while hating fuss and pretentiousness, he never made simpler souls feel uncomfortable or inferior.

His increasing ill-health and his failure to recover after his operation he found irksome, because they interfered with his work, but when he knew there was no hope, he recovered his wonted serenity. When he was near the end he sent me a short note thanking me for a friendship "not bound by the limits of mortality." He has left indeed so abiding a memory that it seems only as if he had gone back for rather longer than usual to his books and his games of patience.

And linking back to these glimpses of Ronald Knox amiably playing the fool with animals, I remembered hearing from a friend of an incident involving his father, the Anglican Bishop of Manchester, which seemed to show that this form of endearing kindliness may have been inherited: When she was a little girl, her puppy died; and to assuage her grief, her mother suggested giving him a funeral, for which she was busily making childish preparations when she saw their neighbor, Bishop Knox, coming along the drive; and her head full of only one possible reason for his presence, ran towards him and called out that he was too early, imagining, of course, that he had come to officiate. A few words aside with her mother enlightened him; he did indeed preside over the puppy's funeral, and she will never forget the appropriate and comforting words he spoke on her "faithful little friend" before the earth was filled in.

Susan Frankau and I usually planned to go together to the Cenacle Convent, high up on Hampstead Heath, whenever Monsignor Knox was due to give a Retreat; and always went through a brief period of panic in case he should be unable to come . . . till we caught our first glimpse of his vivid cyclamen sash between the trees and hedges of the garden, the wearer taking a stroll before we assembled in the chapel for his first Meditation on the same evening; then four on Saturday, four on Sunday, four on Monday, and Tuesday morning we dispersed, resigned to being strangely unable to remember a single word of what he had said, till years later the talks were assembled and published for our avid reading and re-reading: I suppose while he was actually speaking, our attention was too securely locked and sealed in a spell, for memory to function apart. At a private interview during one of these Retreats, Susan reminded him that he had been a Lower Boy at Eton while her husband, Gilbert Frankau, was a lordly senior, probably employing him as a fag and sending him hither and thither on errands.

Well, the stresses change along the years. . . . I went to the Brompton Oratory once to hear a full Nuptial Mass for one of the erstwhile little Aldenham Park girls from the convent school of the Assumption Sisters, where Ronald Knox had been Domestic Chaplain when during the war they were evacuated from Kensington to Shropshire. It was for these fortunate schoolgirls that every week he had delivered his talks on the Mass in Slow Motion and the Creed in Slow Motion; and if years later any of his ex-pupils could persuade him to come along and perform the marriage ceremony and give a personal Address, no one else would do nearly as well. Once that part of it was over and the priest had taken his place to offer the Nuptial Mass, Monsignor Knox withdrew to a prie-dieu at the side of the sanctuary, where he knelt alone and apart, his figure in its purple and white robes and trailing mantle evocative of a great Churchman of medieval days. . . .

And on a perverse slant of memory against which one

is helpless, I suddenly had to recall a small ridiculous episode told of young Father Knox up to tricks, by a nurse
working years ago at St. John's and St. Elizabeth's Hospital: A short while after he had been ordained, he was
visiting another priest convalescent from a serious illness,
and she found the two chuckling like schoolboys over the
havoc they had wrought on the nervous system of the
little ward-maid who came to fetch away the tea-tray;
Ronnie having secretly placed under it one of those rub-
ber gadgets that caused it to wobble and jump up at her
when he squeezed a bulb at the other end!

Back in the Oratory with a silent apology for having
let my attention wander so deplorably from the Business
in Hand, when I remembered—yes, here was the link, and
here distractions might have started—that no Saint was
more addicted to practical joking than St. Philip Neri,
Patron Saint of all Oratorians, who had invented endless
merry tricks to play on his friends and penitents . . . And
there on my right and over the sanctuary was a huge
painted panel depicting this same St. Philip Neri; How
comforting were these discoveries that total irrelevance
need hardly exist within the Catholic Church.

Leaving the Oratory, and now not quite in the mood
for a crowded wedding reception, I asked my escort to
deliver a message to Monsignor Knox, who might like to
hear that Gilbert Frankau had just been received into the
Church. A couple of days later I had a note from Ronald
Knox asking if the message were true? If true, would I
forward Gilbert the enclosed letter? Curiosity could
hardly bear not to be in on what one Old Etonian had
found to say to another; and recently Susan allowed me
to share the delicious irony of a heavenly doodle traced
by the years.

("I can't see anything *ironic* about it," Ronald Knox would no doubt have remarked at this juncture, his understanding always so quick and sensitive to take a point unless it happened to redound to his own aggrandizement!)

Dear Frankau,
    —I hope this address is not unsuitable, as coming from a school-fellow, and a reader, in its day, of the X. I got a message on Saturday as from G. B. Stern, to tell me that you have at last stepped under the ropes into the enclosure. I hope this is true. It's odd how easy it seems, *being* a Catholic, when it seemed so hard to *become* one; how even the latecomer feels as if he'd been there all his life! . . . But it's a bit lonely for some people. I said Mass for you this morning, and will go on remembering your intentions. Don't answer this.
                    Yours sincerely,
                    R. A. KNOX.

"Dear Frankau" and (in spite of "don't answer this") "Dear Knox," profoundly honored at the notice taken of him by a small and presumably grubby junior who used to scamper about to do his bidding; again and again Gilbert could have been heard proudly boasting "As my friend Monsignor Ronald Knox said to me in a personal letter. . . ."
    But like Gilbert, I too have been given something to boast about, and find it difficult not to linger on the accolade: "You always put me on to things I'd never run into before" in a letter thanking me for a book of mine. He went on with a wonderful description of a dream he had had, with all the Lewis Carroll properties:

Don't you think this would make rather a good dream?—You are waiting on a platform at Paddington, and it's past time for the train to start, but it hasn't even come into the station. Then the Archbishop of Canterbury comes up, and explains that it can't get out of its siding, because an engine has run off the lines just in front of it. The odd thing is that that is what happened to me in real life, the day before yesterday.

And he ended with: "It was very good of you to send me the book, and I won't defend myself about the sunbeam." For according to his essay on St. Chad, this was the only Saint known to have used a sunbeam as a clothes-horse; yet in those enchanting chronicles of the Saints where simple idiocy combines with a fully integrated quality which in the radiance of pure white contains all the primary colors of the spectrum, I had discovered that St. Bridget of Kildare was also said to have flung her cloak over a ray of sunlight when she had just been drenched in a shower of rain. When I first broke it to him, after a moment's stunned silence he took refuge in a typical defense: "Oh, she was just a woman; they'd hang their clothes anywhere!" And though he wrote, "I won't defend myself about the sunbeam," he had not quite surrendered priority, for in a postscript he continued the argument:

But Saints *do* duplicate one another's performances. I observed the other day that when Gerard Groote (author?? of the *Imitation*) was dying, he told his religious it was a good thing he should die, because then he would be able to shower roses on them.

Fortunately the question marks did not puzzle me to the verge of begging for elucidation: for an indignant partisan of the theory that Thomas à Kempis had merely been entrusted later with the task of translating Gerard Groote's *Imitation of Christ* into Latin, had sent me a copy to prove her contention. Nevertheless I had become acclimatized to Thomas à Kempis as the original author of the *Imitation*, and perhaps in the same unenterprising spirit by which I had become acclimatized to Purcell as the composer of the Trumpet Voluntary whereas it was really Jeremiah Clarke, I was pleased to interpret Ronald Knox's two question marks as a sign that he too stood out for the claims of Thomas à Kempis; though doubtless on a more scholarly basis of argument than my own indolent "You see, I've got so used to the name!"

As for his reference to St. Thérèse and her shower of roses, I shall always treasure an allusion to the young Carmelite nun, when he was defining the adjective "simple," as "perfectly integrated;" St. Thérèse, he remarked, had not wasted her energy as most of us do, exploring along a hundred tracks with self blocking the vista at the end of each; all she thought and said and did was gathered in towards one end and purpose; people were wont to say a little contemptuously: "Oh, she's just a *child*, you know!" ... Just a child, harmlessly pleased with her babyish playthings, her little simple rubrics . . . and then he added with a side-long glance at his audience: "Have you ever known a *child* like St. Thérèse?" And chapel or no chapel (for his talk took place at a Convent Retreat) everyone burst out laughing. No, we had never known a child like St. Thérèse!

In a preface to a special edition of Father Brown, Monsignor Knox spoke of G. K. Chesterton as likewise "perfectly integrated, having a philosophy of life—and not of this life only, which was all of a piece." It may be that the physical difference between Chesterton and St. Thérèse had prevented him from noticing the double significance of this illustration which he introduced in different essays at different times; for if he *had* noticed how he was accidentally proving their essential resemblance, the writer in him must have sat up and with an exultant whoop given thanks for treasure trove, as writers (and converts) sometimes do find treasure when they are not looking for it. No one in their senses could possibly suspect such a brilliant wit and *savant* and satirist as Monsignor Ronald Knox of being duped by the merely chocolate-box appeal of those ubiquitous statues where a young nun holds in her hand a trail of roses, symbolic of her intention to let them fall to earth in a pretty shower of scent and petals; yet he had chosen to re-translate her *Histoire d'une Âme* for his last task on earth; and at the annual Romanes Lecture at Oxford in 1957, he mentioned that it had not been altogether easy to imagine himself into the mind and heart and soul of the little Carmelite and to achieve by empathy her true intentions . . .

Nor are we surprised that under her protection he was able to finish his translation; not surprised, but exultant at such a lenient working-out of the usually inexorable pattern of life and death.

I went to bed early on the night of August 24, 1957, tired out from a day of wild gales; it did not matter that the electricity had failed, because wanting to listen to Brahms' Fourth Symphony to be relayed from Edinburgh after the nine o'clock news on the Home Service, a soft night light was all the illumination I needed. To be certain of not missing one note of it, I turned on my battery set a few minutes early, just in time to hear an impersonal voice state that "the death has occurred of Monsignor Ronald Knox." . . .

Hors concours. Hors de combat.

Had I thus arranged to be alone in a setting of dim light and the perfect Requiem music to follow the announcement, had it been within one's power to devise such appropriate incidentals, they would have been of course an intolerable affectation; yet happening to receive the benison thus fortuitously, and moreover only some seven or eight years since I had learnt to love Brahms, and not even all of Brahms, but especially *this*. . . . I accepted it gratefully.

After the slow movement, I switched off, and discovered that meanwhile the electricity had returned as though adapting itself to my need of reading Ronald Knox's own reactions to the subject of death and the fear of death in his *Retreat for Lay People*: I reached out for it, and found:

> This separating of soul and body is the nearest thing to annihilation which it is ours to give. Let us look forward, then, to death, as the moment at which we shall make to God the supreme confession of our creatureliness; when we shall immolate, in honor of Him this candle, to be blown out. The dearer a thing life seems to you, the harder it seems to relinquish, the more motive for generosity in offering it.

If I were only allowed one word to summarize the value to me of six or seven bedside volumes by Ronald Knox

—and in the cause of austerity it might be a good notion
if indeed only one word were allowed for describing the
books we care for most!—I should choose *indispensable*,
instead of enlarging on them in more glowing, less pedestrian terms. His thoughts illumine the darkness, and he
might have sent me in a steep bill for spiritual repairs and
renewals engendered by my constant insatiable re-reading of *Retreat for Lay People* and (perhaps astonishingly)
Retreat for Priests, and of the three Slow Motion books:
*The Mass in Slow Motion, The Creed in Slow Motion,
The Gospel in Slow Motion;* and *The Window in the
Wall* and *Heaven and Charing Cross.* He himself looked
on *Enthusiasm* as his best work, but so far I have eyed it respectfully and left it at a safe distance from my beside,
as no tender companion for one's slowed-up hours; but I
should certainly have included in my desiderata to be la-
beled "Wanted on Voyage," the *Selection from the occasional Sermons of the Right Reverend Monsignor Ronald
Arbuthnott Knox; sometime Scholar of Balliol College and
Fellow of Trinity College, Oxford; Domestic Prelate to
His Holiness the Pope, Edited by Evelyn Waugh and
published in a limited edition by the Dropmore Press,* if all
this magnificence could come down in the world and be
re-issued small and modest and light for bedside handling.
For years we speak of our "bedside books" meaning just
a hand lazily stretched out in the early morning or for
half-an-hour's browsing before going to sleep. . . . It is
only when we are quietly nearing our end that they come
to be accepted as bedside for both day and night, allied
no less reassuringly than sleep and death.

And I recalled a phrase peculiar to him and recurring
over and over again in his letters: "Don't forget to signal
when you come to these parts" . . . "Remember you must

signal when you come down." One's personal reactions
to grief are often foolish and inexplicable, or why should
it now strike me so poignantly when, after all, it was quite
an ordinary variation on "mind you let me know," only
become haunting when echoed from distances inaccessi-
ble: "Don't forget to signal. . . ."

The last time I had seen him was towards the end of
one of his Cenacle Retreats. I forget why I thought I had
to leave before supper on the Monday evening and so miss
his final talk, instead of letting the Retreat complete itself
and depart with the others on Tuesday morning after
breakfast; I hope at least it may have been for a fairly
adequate reason, say of sparing someone a disappointment
by cancelling a date made a long time previously, and not
merely a monstrous failure of my sense of proportion in
deliberately precipitating a loss which no prayer to St.
Anthony—"Cher St. Antoine de Pavie, rends moi ce que
j'ai perdu"—could ever recover.

Monsignor's arrival in the chapel to give us his four
o'clock Meditation had been preceded by an unusually
long delay; we wondered anxiously what had happened,
whether he were suddenly taken ill, and if so, why had
not one of the nuns come to tell us? Then at last he did
appear, apologetic and out of breath, and explained how
the door and window of his study had been accidentally
left wide open and a high wind blown in, so that returning to fetch the MS. of the talk he intended to give us,
he had found all his papers whirling round the floor in
a wild saraband instead of as he had left them, neatly prepared on his desk; they were in such confusion that after
trying to chase and re-assemble them, he had had to abandon the attempt, and would therefore substitute a talk

that perhaps some of us had heard before at some earlier
Retreat, an old meditation, not the one freshly minted
which he had planned to give us.

Our relief at seeing him well and on his feet naturally
could not find vent by any burst of applause, so in attentive silence we settled down to listen.

Later, while I was standing in the entrance hall saying
good-bye to Mother Thornton and leaving a message for
Monsignor Knox, he passed through the hall himself, and
halted on seeing my suitcase: "You're not going?"

"Yes, I'm afraid I have to; I do wish I needn't, but I
promised—" and so forth.

"But I'll be giving you a *new* talk tonight," Ronnie explained, terribly remorseful at his flagrant misdemeanor,
"not one that you've heard already"; conceding as a matter of course that it was so dreadful of him just once to
have robbed us of our due, that it would have been natural for me in consequence to have left the Retreat before
the end; and he repeated in mounting distress: "It won't
be another old one tonight." No trace of resentment or
wounded pride, but as though for this service and no
other, he existed.

Yet though I have lost for ever an hour of treasure ir-
replaceable, I recognized even then that contracted to the
size of a pocket dictionary definition, small and clear, I
had been given treasure in a different idiom: a glimpse
of humility come true. And in his own words when we
came away from Baron von Hügel's almost anonymous
little grave, it was rather impressive.

INDEX

DATE DUE

MAY 31 1994	

DEMCO, INC. 38-2931